PICASSO, BRAQUE, GRIS, LÉGER

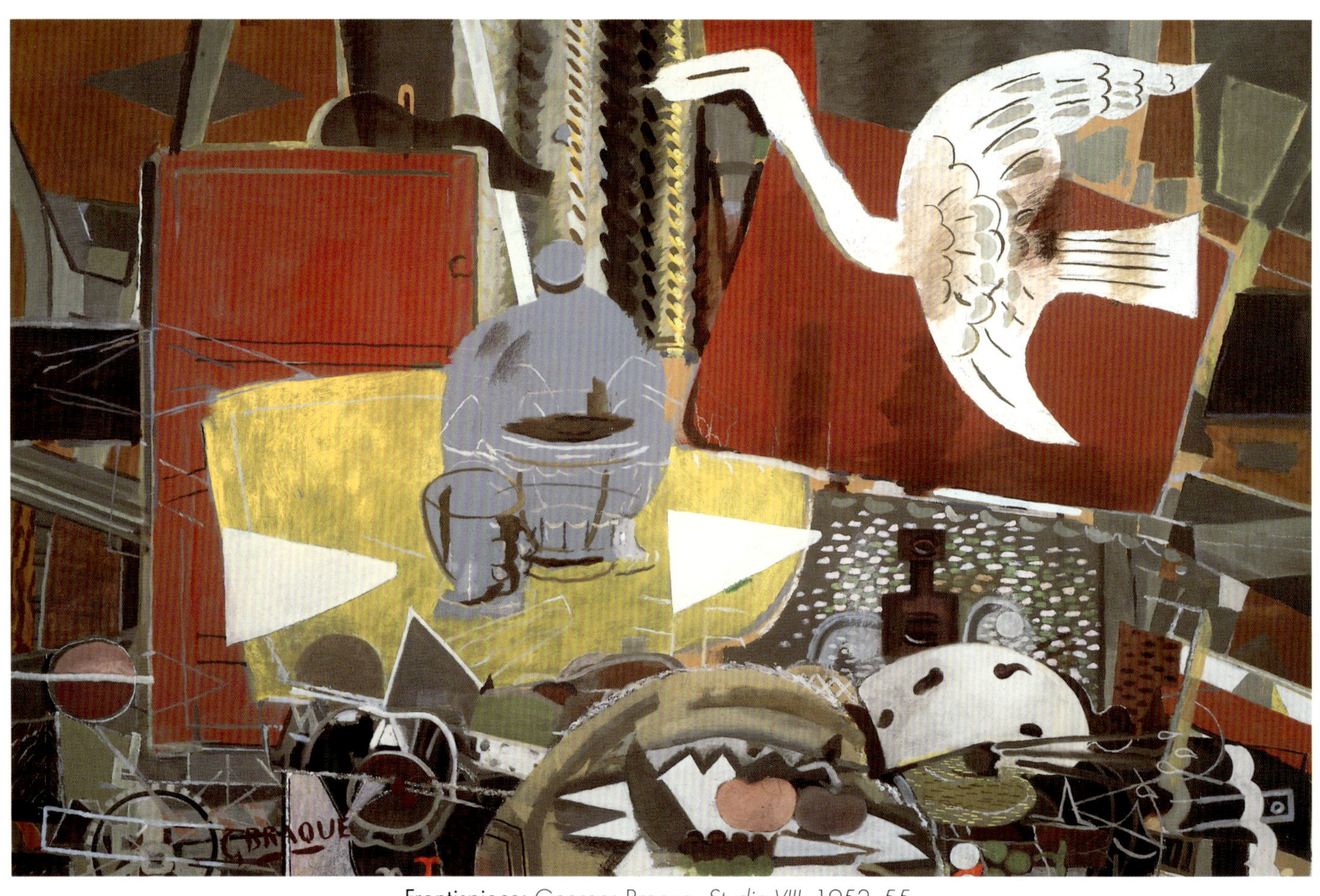

Frontispiece: Georges Braque, *Studio VIII*, 1952–55
oil on canvas, 52 × 77½ in. (132.1 × 196.9 cm.), private collection. (Photo, John Webb.)

PICASSO, BRAQUE, GRIS, LÉGER

DOUGLAS COOPER COLLECTING CUBISM

DOROTHY M. KOSINSKI

THE MUSEUM OF FINE ARTS, HOUSTON

Published by The Museum of Fine Arts, Houston
on the occasion of the exhibition
Picasso, Braque, Gris, Léger
Douglas Cooper Collecting Cubism

The Museum of Fine Arts, Houston
October 14, 1990 – December 30, 1990

Standard Book Number: 0-89090-049-3
Library of Congress Catalogue Card Number: 90-053298

Library of Congress Cataloging-in-Publication Data

Kosinski, Dorothy M.
Picasso, Braque, Gris, Léger: Douglas Cooper collecting Cubism / essay by Dorothy M. Kosinski: the Museum of Fine Arts, Houston, October 14, 1990 – December 30, 1990
p. cm.
Exhibition catalog.
Includes bibliographical references.
ISBN 0-89090-049-3 (pbk.)
1. Cubism — France — Exhibitions. 2. Art, Modern — 20th Century — France — Exhibitions. 3. Art, French — Exhibitions. 4. Cooper, Douglas, 1911– — Art collections — Exhibitions. 5. Art — Private collections — Exhibitions. 6. Cooper, Douglas, 1911– — Art patronage — Exhibitions. I. Museum of Fine Arts, Houston. II. Title. N6848.5.C82K67 1990
759.4′074′7641411 — dc20 90–53298
CIP

Editor: Mary Christian
Production Manager: Kathryn L. Kelley
Assistant Editor: Michelle Nichols
Designer: Peter Layne

Cover: Pablo Picasso, *Three Figures under a Tree*, winter 1907–08, oil on canvas, 39 × 39 in. (99 × 99 cm.), Musée Picasso, Paris.

This exhibition is made possible in Houston
by generous grants from

Mrs. Theodore N. Law

Mr. and Mrs. Meredith J. Long

The Brown Foundation, Inc.

Louisa Stude Sarofim

Mr. and Mrs. James A. Elkins, Jr.

Goldman, Sachs & Co.

Isabell and Max Herzstein

Janie C. Lee

Mr. and Mrs. Wallace S. Wilson

Cushman Realty Corporation

Continental Airlines

This exhibition is supported by an indemnity from the
Federal Council on the Arts and the Humanities.

LENDERS TO THE EXHIBITION

Jean-Claude Bellier, Paris

Dr. and Mme. Antoine Benedittini, France

The Douglas Cooper Collection, Churchglade Ltd.

The Fogg Art Museum, Harvard University
Cambridge, Massachusetts

Galerie Louise Leiris, Paris

Jasper Johns

Kunstmuseum Basel

William McCarty-Cooper

The Metropolitan Museum of Art, New York

Musée Picasso, Paris

Museo del Prado, Madrid

John Richardson

Thyssen-Bornemisza Collection, Lugano, Switzerland

The Museum of Ulm, Permanent Loan from the State of Baden-Württemberg
Federal Republic of Germany

Private collections

AUTHOR'S ACKNOWLEDGMENTS

The essay in this catalogue presents an in-depth and detailed history of the formation of Douglas Cooper's collection in the 1930s. This work builds upon the more general presentation of Cooper and his collection which I wrote for the Basel/London/Philadelphia exhibition of 1987–88. It is part, moreover, of a larger project now underway, a history and complete catalogue of Cooper's entire collection. Cooper's story will play a role, as well, in another publication project, only now in its incipient stages, dealing with the reception and patronage of the Cubists. None of these projects would have come to pass were it not for the generous and animating support of William McCarty-Cooper, and it is to him that I dedicate this catalogue.

Needless to say, I am very grateful for the interest of the Museum of Fine Arts, Houston in Cooper and their suggestion to sponsor this exhibition and catalogue. I extend my thanks especially to Peter C. Marzio, director; David B. Warren, associate director; and Alison de Lima Greene, associate curator, twentieth-century art. I would also like to thank Shannon Halwes for her assistance in assembling material for the catalogue, Wanda Allison, Carrie Springer, Karen Bremer, Charles Carroll, Sara Garcia, Celeste Marie Adams, Mary Christian, Michelle Nichols, Kathryn Kelley, Susan Giannantonio, Jack Eby, Lorri Lewis, Margaret Skidmore, Barbara Michels, Anne Rosen, and Anne Lewis. I am also grateful for the support and interest of two members of the Houston community: Janie C. Lee and Sue Rowan Pittman.

I am indebted to John Richardson for his continued generosity with information and ideas about Cooper and to Angelica Rudenstine for her generous help and sound advice. I am grateful, too, to Leonard Lauder for his interest in and support of this project. My thanks as well to his curator, Emily Braun, for her assistance.

I wish to thank, as well, my assistants, Caroline Brooke and Lysa Hochroth, for their good work.

Many individuals were extremely generous to us with information, memories, and materials. I wish to thank: Jean-Pierre Bénézit, Galerie Bénézit, Paris; Maurice Covo, Galerie Renou & Poyet, Paris; Christian Derouet, Musée National d'Art Moderne, Centre Georges Pompidou, Paris; Elisabeth Eichmann, Vienna; Jean-François Jaeger, Paris; John Livingood, Paris; Albert Loeb, Galerie Loeb, Paris; James Mayor, The Mayor Gallery, London; Mrs. Fred H. Mayor; Christoph Pudelko, Galerie Pudelko, Bonn; Angela Rosengart, Luzerne; Helène Seckel, Musée Picasso, Paris.

I am indebted to the staffs of the Getty Center for the History of Art and the Humanities, Santa Monica, and the Museum of Modern Art Library, New York.

No exhibition comes to pass without the generosity of its lenders. I extend my thanks to all of them and especially to Churchglade Ltd. for their crucial support.

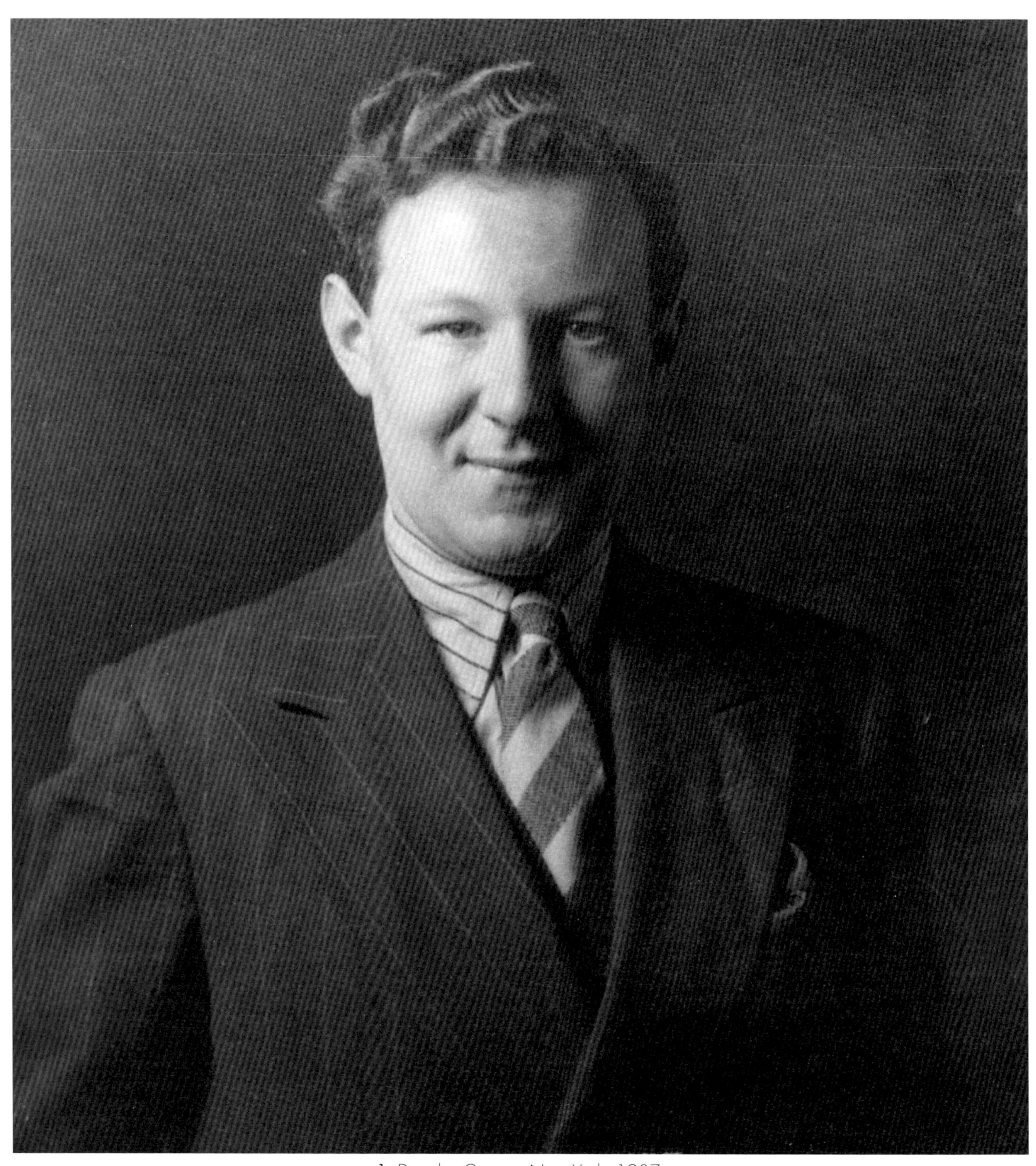

1. Douglas Cooper, New York, 1937
(Photo, Associated News, Photographic Service, Inc.)

FOREWORD

THE ADVENTURE OF A LIFETIME

Writing in 1983, after fifty years of passionate collecting, Douglas Cooper (1911–1984) recalled the climate of the art world in post-Depression Europe:

> *This was the situation at the beginning of the 1930s, as I discovered for myself when I first began to be deeply involved with twentieth-century art, and in particular with the painting of the true Cubists. It was a favourable moment for a collector to buy because the earlier boom had turned into a terrible and long-lasting slump, with the result that the prices for paintings by the four masters of Cubism had again fallen, having been pushed upwards in the later 1920s by a growing demand for the American market. I took advantage of the situation for myself as best I could and in 1932 began to buy true Cubist paintings with the intention of forming a substantial collection of my own. The pursuit became for me the adventure of a lifetime and led to my coming to know not only the artists concerned (apart from Gris, who was already dead) but also a great many...dealers and collectors.*[1]

In 1932 Cooper, a young English art historian and connoisseur, had come into a generous inheritance, one-third of which he decided to devote to collecting art. Cubism was by then a well-established movement, one that no longer generated the fervid controversy that greeted the "geometrical schemes" and "cubes" of 1908.[2] The passionate defense of Cubism voiced by its first proponents — the poet and critic Guillaume Apollinaire, the collector and dealer Daniel-Henry Kahnweiler, not to mention the artists themselves — had given way to the first serious efforts to catalogue the creative outpouring of the volatile first decades of the twentieth century. For example, 1932 saw the publication of the first volume of Christian Zervos' *catalogue raisonné* of Pablo Picasso.

By the early 1930s it was the turn of a third generation of collectors to investigate Cubist art. World financial crises had forced many earlier collectors to give up their paintings and drawings, thus enabling emerging experts like Cooper to acquire outstanding works of art. Cooper was well aware that he was following in the footsteps of the pioneering efforts of the American collectors Gertrude Stein and John Quinn, as well as the brilliant early dealer-collectors Wilhelm Uhde, Ambroise Vollard, and Kahnweiler. The later enthusiasts of the 1920s, including Léonce Rosenberg, Alfred Flechtheim, Dr. G.F. Reber, and Katherine Dreier, were also well known to him.[3] Indeed, as Dr. Dorothy Kosinski demonstrates in her essay for this catalogue, Cooper worked closely with many of these figures, proving to be one of the most astute collectors of his generation.

This exhibition of the former Cooper collection focuses on the first decade of Cooper's activities and has been conceived as a sequel to the 1987 exhibition *Douglas Cooper und die Meister des Kubismus,* sponsored by the Kunstmuseum Basel and organized by Dr. Kosinski, curator of The Douglas Cooper Collection.[4] The Museum of Fine Arts, Houston invited Dr. Kosinski to rethink and expand her first study of Douglas Cooper. The concept for the current presentation is embodied in the last footnote to her introduction of the Basel catalogue: "An exhibition which would reassemble Cooper's collection beginning in the thirties and follow its subsequent refinement, is a project of a different scope, involving complex detective work tracing the many works which have been dispersed over the years."[5] Thanks to several years of detection, as well as to the outstanding generosity of our lenders, we now have the opportunity to understand more fully Cooper's collecting method. While the majority of works in our exhibition document Cooper's purchases of the 1930s, certain key later drawings and paintings have been included as well.

The introductory essay of the Basel catalogue is exceptionally comprehensive, giving us a fascinating picture of Cooper's scholarship and collecting activities. Like many great collectors, Cooper was captivated by the art of collecting and wrote extensively on the efforts of his predecessors in this area.[6] However, he modestly omitted any detailed description of his own efforts in this direction, a lacuna that has been filled by Dr. Kosinski's research. For the purposes of this introduction, it is worth summarizing the distinctive characteristics that set Cooper apart from his colleagues.

Cooper's nationality, youth, and focus on what he later called the "essential Cubists" (Pablo Picasso, Georges Braque, Juan Gris, and Fernand Léger) made him a unique figure among the collectors of the 1930s. Unlike many of the first supporters of Cubism, Cooper did not take up permanent residence in Paris. Although he frequently crossed the channel, he maintained an apartment in London until 1952, when he moved to the South of France. Yet in London he was something of an anomaly since, as he frequently noted in his writings, England produced no great collectors of Cubism:

> *The taste of the English in modern art, until about 1939, was for Bonnard, Vuillard, Rouault, post-1918 Matisse, Derain, Modigliani, and Utrillo, artists who had been accepted in the Fry-Bell circle before 1920. Modern art, in order to be acceptable, had to appear traditional, decorative, and easy to understand. Thus no one collected Fauve or Cubist pictures; very occasionally single pictures by Picasso, Braque, or Juan Gris might be bought by a collector, virtually never by a museum.*[7]

However, Cooper did find one mentor in England, albeit one who did not collect Cubist art. Samuel Courtauld, the great collector of Post-Impressionist paintings, was a friend of Cooper's uncle, and the young Cooper had been introduced to Courtauld by about 1924, when Cooper was thirteen. From Courtauld, Cooper learned to follow the development of a select group of masters, a method he rigorously applied to his own collecting activities.

Cooper's youth is easy to overlook until one sees a photograph of him with his colleagues: in 1932 he was twenty-one. As was typical, he had received his inheritance upon reaching his majority. The artists he admired were financially established and well into their careers: Léger and Picasso were fifty-one, Braque fifty. Similarly, Kahnweiler was forty-eight and Gertrude Stein ten years his senior. This difference in age probably saved Cooper from the combative relationships that many of the first collectors experienced with the Cubist painters. The boon of his inheritance further allowed him to treat collecting as an enterprise, one that he pursued with unflagging enthusiasm.

As Dr. Kosinski has documented step-by-step, Cooper developed his collection with exceptional sureness, single-mindedly focusing on what he later identified as "true Cubism" or the "essential Cubism." Cooper was frequently wide-ranging in his research, and his monumental exhibition *The Cubist Epoch* (1970) was generous in its survey of all aspects of the Cubist movement, both in and outside of Paris.[8] However, in collecting he largely concentrated on amassing representative works by Braque, Picasso, Gris, and Léger, artists who he felt were the creators of the Cubist idiom. Cooper refused to define Cubism according to a set formula, emphasizing instead the distinctive qualities in the work of these artists. In 1983 he proposed with his coauthor Gary Tinterow that in the final analysis Cubism "cannot be defined as a style any more than it can be identified by its subject matter. Nor was it the expression in pictorial terms of any particular philosophy. By their very nature...Cubist paintings are essentially personal in character and bear the mark of an individual personality."[9]

It was, perhaps, this nuanced understanding of Cubism that made Cooper a great collector. As the works in this exhibition demonstrate, Cooper was attentive to the individual character of each artist and the collection as a whole gives us a richly complex overview of the formative years of the Cubist avant-garde and its later evolution. Cooper sought out not only paintings that offer telling insight into a key moment in the history of Cubism — Picasso's *Three Figures under a Tree* (1907–08, checklist 54) and Georges Braque's *Studio VIII* (1952–55, checklist 8), for example, can be seen as the alpha and omega of his collection — but he also brought together more ephemeral and personal sketches and studies, such as Léger's riveting ink drawing from the trenches, *Two Dead* (1916, checklist 31), and Gris's remarkable copies after Cézanne (1916, checklist 20 and 21).

Cooper's philosophy of collecting and his championship of artists were perhaps most passionately stated in a 1964 editorial published in *The Times*

Literary Supplement. After reflecting on the past generations of the avant-garde that survived despite the "tastes and ideas of officialdom," Cooper wrote:

> *Yet society was ultimately the loser, because on account of its philistinism it failed to harness the great original talents which were at its disposal to work for the benefit of the community as a whole. For between 1840 and 1940 there was a creative outburst in Europe which can justifiably be compared with that of the Italian Renaissance. And given enlightened patronage during those years it should have been possible to transform and ennoble the face of Europe.*[10]

While he could not claim that he had "transformed the face of Europe," Cooper's years of enlightened patronage, his enormous contribution to the written scholarship of modern art, and the many exhibitions he organized have certainly established a permanent contribution to our community as a whole. The Museum of Fine Arts, Houston welcomes the opportunity to make this collection known to a broader public. We thank Dr. Kosinski for the wonderful work she has contributed to this project and William McCarty-Cooper for his enthusiastic support.

Alison de Lima Greene

Associate Curator
The Museum of Fine Arts, Houston

1 Douglas Cooper, "Early Purchasers of True Cubist Art," in *The Essential Cubism: Braque, Picasso and Their Friends, 1907–1920* (with Gary Tinterow), London, The Tate Gallery, 1983, p. 31. See also Dorothy Kosinski, *Douglas Cooper und die Meister des Kubismus,* Basel, Kunstmuseum, 1987, pp. 17–18.

2 The Paris art critic Louis Vauxcelles was the first to refer to this new style in terms of "cubes" in his review of Georges Braque's exhibition at the Galerie Kahnweiler in 1908. See "Exposition Braque," *Gil Blas* (Paris), November 14, 1908; rpt. in Edward F. Fry, *Cubism* (New York: McGraw-Hill Book Company, 1966), pp. 50–51.

3 See Cooper, "Early Purchasers of True Cubist Art," pp. 15–31 for a detailed description of the first generations of Cubist collectors.

4 The Douglas Cooper Collection, owned and supported in part by Churchglade Ltd., as well as by other private individuals, maintains a small group of works selected from the original collection. It also sponsors research and documentation of Cooper's contribution as a collector, art historian, and critic.

5 Kosinski, p. 56, note 63.

6 Cooper, "Early Purchasers of True Cubist Art," pp. 15–31; see also Cooper, "Gertrude Stein and Juan Gris," in *Four Americans in Paris,* New York, The Museum of Modern Art, 1970, pp. 65–73.

7 Cooper, *The Courtauld Collection* (London: University of London, Athlone Press, 1954), p. 59; cited in Kosinski, p. 15.

8 Organized by the Los Angeles County Museum of Art and the Metropolitan Museum of Art, New York, 1970–71.

9 Cooper and Tinterow, "Introduction," *The Essential Cubism,* p. 14.

10 Cooper, "Establishment and Avant-garde," *The Times Literary Supplement* (London), September 3, 1964, p. 823.

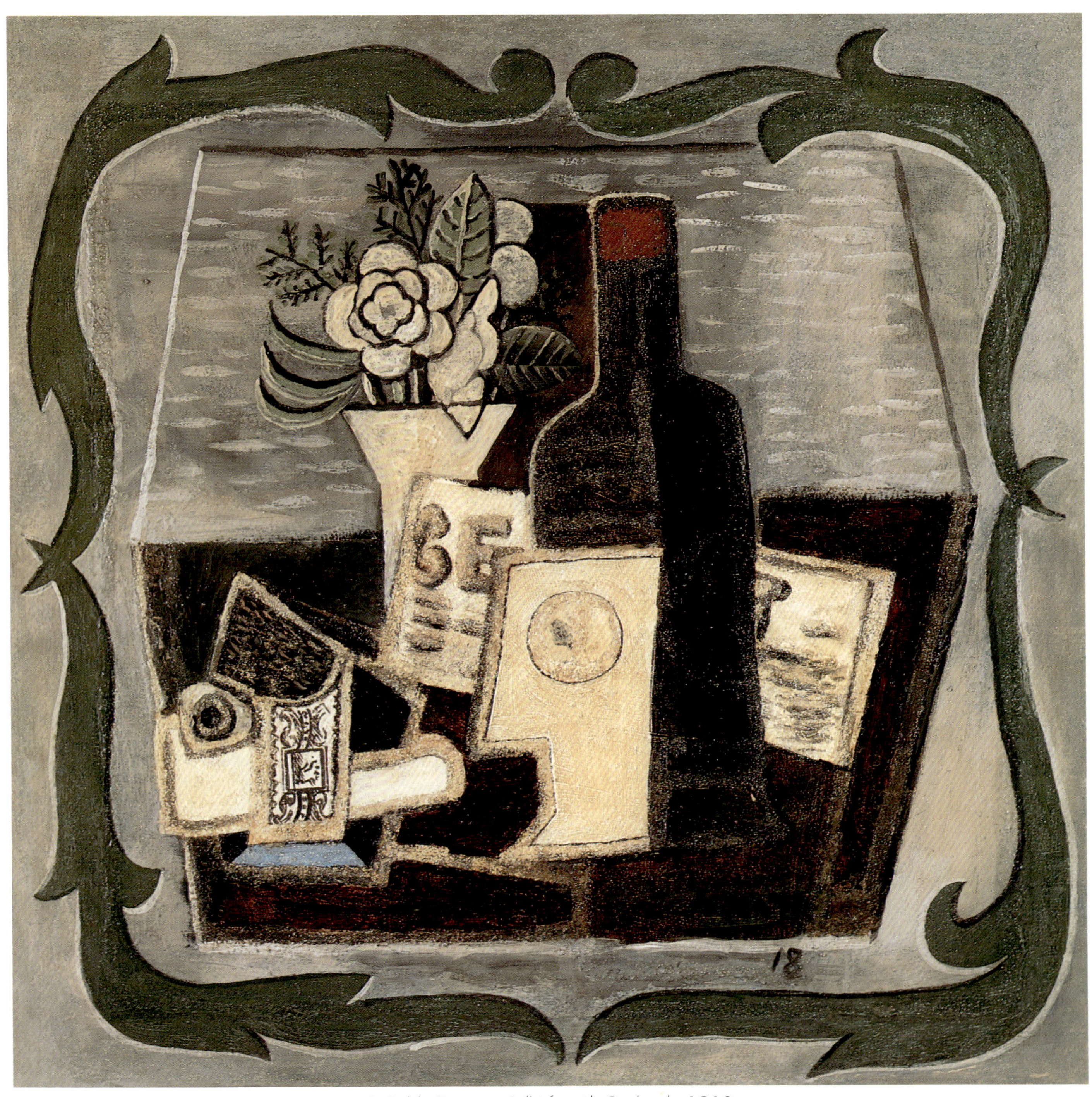

2. Pablo Picasso, *Still Life with Garlands*, 1918
oil and sand on canvas, 18 3/16 × 18 1/8 in. (46.1 × 46 cm.), private collection.

PICASSO, BRAQUE, GRIS, LÉGER
DOUGLAS COOPER COLLECTING CUBISM

The story of the initial years of Douglas Cooper's collecting during the 1930s is astounding because of how rapidly and intensely he launched the enterprise. From spring of 1933 until late summer of 1939, Cooper invested about £10,000 to purchase about 128 works of art, and he acquired seven additional works as gifts, some of these from the artists themselves.[1] Within a mere six years he managed to establish the core of his important Cubist collection, amassing the pictures that were to remain the heart of the collection for more than four decades until Cooper's death in 1984. This feat was accomplished during a period of tremendous socio-political upheaval. The key events of the dramatic backdrop of that decade are familiar: the economic instability following the world financial crash of 1929 and 1930, Hitler's rise to power in 1933 and the subsequent increasing militarization of Germany, the annexation of Austria in 1938 and Czechoslovakia in 1939, and, finally, the outbreak of war in September 1939. The significance of the economic and political factors in this period indicates how the purely financial details of Cooper's collecting activities are relevant to the context of this study. For this reason, all known prices that Cooper paid are cited here in the text.[2]

The configuration of Cooper's purchases from these years reveals a clarity of vision and a sound philosophical base that transcends financial advantage. His most important acquisitions included seven works by Georges Braque, twenty-seven by Juan Gris, thirty-nine by Fernand Léger, and thirty-six by Pablo Picasso. In a scant six years, then, Cooper fulfilled the program that he had established in 1932: to devote a significant portion of his recent inheritance to form a comprehensive collection of Cubist works of art. The collection was comprehensive in the sense that it featured the four "true" Cubists — Braque, Gris, Léger, and Picasso — in their development from 1906 to 1914. Rather than maintaining the more typical focus on oil paintings and great masterworks, Cooper sought out all of these artists' primary media, including paintings, drawings, *papiers collés*, prints, and sculptures. Moreover, he included the full range of subject matter, with the artists' figural, landscape, and still-life compositions. In addition to these Cubist works, Cooper made twenty-seven documented acquisitions that include twenty works by Joan Miró.[3] While outside the focus of this catalogue and exhibition, these holdings make clear Cooper's sincere enthusiasm for the Spaniard's work as well as his cordial relationship with the artist. More importantly, this appreciation of Miró, as well as Cooper's demonstrated enthusiasm for the 1930s works of Picasso, Braque, and Léger, reveals an animated engagement in the contemporary avant-garde. This was coupled with, or even inspired by, a firm rejection of what Cooper considered to be the moribund state of contemporary art in his native England.

THE MAYOR GALLERY

Cooper's involvement in the world of art took concrete form with his role as one of the directors of the Mayor Gallery in London from 1933 until 1937 or 1938. In Fred Hoyland Mayor (1903-1973), Cooper found an experienced guide to, and fellow enthusiast for, the contemporary avant-garde (fig. 3).[4] As early as 1925 Mayor had directed a gallery on Cork Street in London that specialized in modern English and French art including, notably in this context, works by Picasso, Léger, and Gris.[5] The following year he expanded the gallery, adding a branch on Sackville Street. Mayor's short-lived venture was heralded in the press for presenting artists otherwise neglected in England at that time.[6] Despite this recognition, however, in 1926 the gallery on Sackville Street closed in bankruptcy. Mayor subsequently ran a gallery for the London Arts Association, backed by Maynard Keynes and Arnold Bennett, that primarily represented Bloomsbury artists. This venture was followed by his stint, beginning in 1929, as the director of a gallery jointly owned by Paul Guillaume and Brandon Davis. Thus Mayor's commitment to the avant-garde was already demonstrated well before he opened his gallery on Cork Street in 1933. This new gallery was backed by Cooper (who reportedly invested £2,000 in the gallery at the onset) and by J.F. (Fyfe) Duthie,

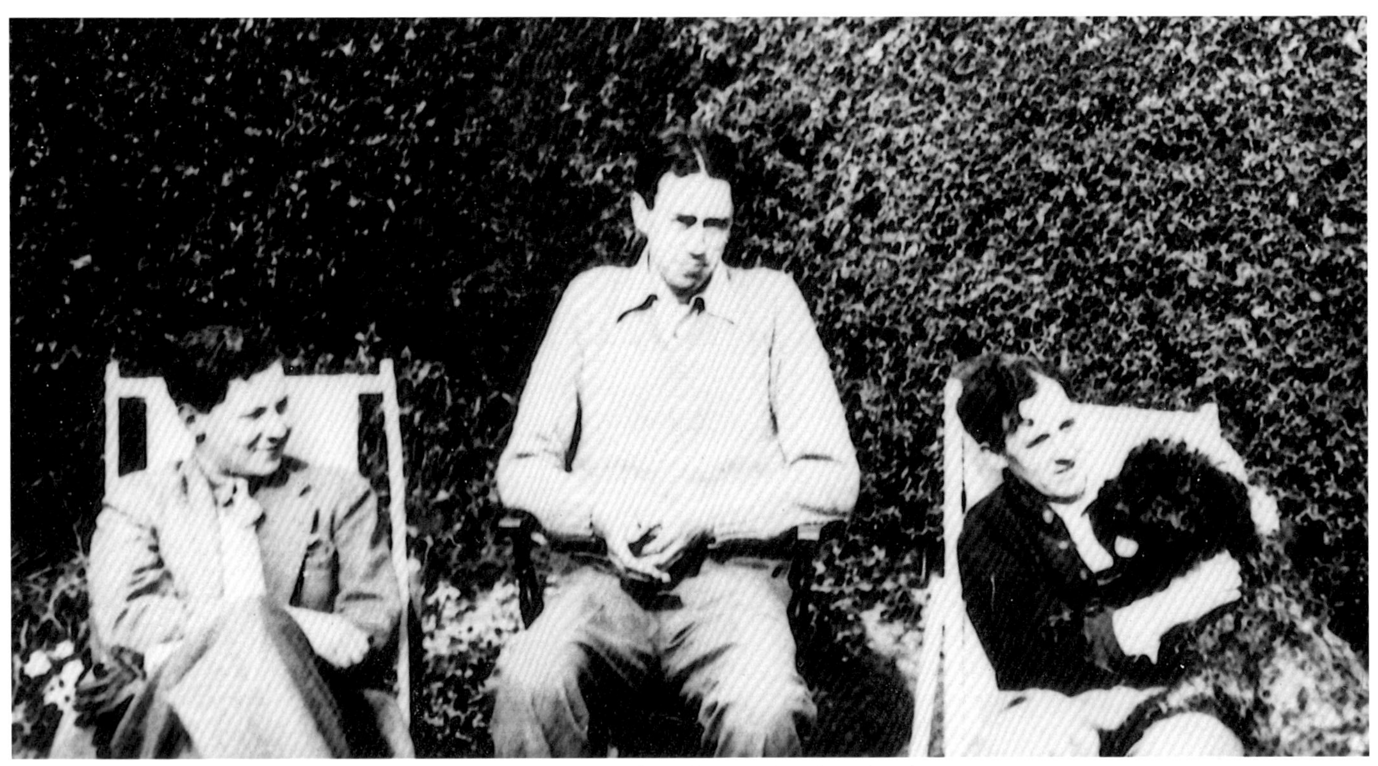

3. Douglas Cooper, J. Fyfe Duthie, and Fred Hoyland Mayor,
partners of the Mayor Gallery, c. 1933. (Photo, courtesy Barbara Wadsworth.)

a long-time friend of Mayor. What Mayor lacked in financial means he made up for in experience; through his earlier ventures he had acquired broad and invaluable contacts with dealers, galleries, and collectors throughout Europe, but most importantly in Paris.

Mayor probably met Cooper through the circle of modern artists in England whom Mayor promoted, which included the Australian Roy de Maistre and the South African Teddy Wolfe.[7] The meeting between Mayor and Cooper might also have been initiated by John Weyman, who was a young collector, another member of this circle, and a close friend of both de Maistre and Cooper.[8] Although it might seem that Mayor and Cooper could have created an ideal partnership from their combined interests, money, and experience, only a short time passed before their relationship went awry. Cooper increasingly focused his interest and effort on the growth of his own collection rather than on the success of the Mayor Gallery.

The opening exhibition at the Mayor Gallery on April 20, 1933 included works by major British and European artists. The roster of participants included the four Cubist artists under discussion here, in addition to Francis Bacon, Max Ernst, Paul Klee, Jean Lurçat, André Masson, Jean Metzinger, Joan Miró, Henry Moore, Paul Nash, Ben Nicholson, Francis Picabia, Leopold Survage, and Ossip Zadkine.[9] These artists reflected the commitment to the English and French avant-garde that had informed Mayor's early gallery ventures. This exhibition was followed by one-person shows devoted to works by Ernst and Miró. The year ended with an exhibition of drawings by Tristram Hillier, Wassily Kandinsky, Nash, and Zadkine.

The Mayor Gallery was influential, as well, as headquarters of Unit One, a loose association of contemporary British artists. This group included the sculptors Henry Moore and Barbara Hepworth; the painters Edward Wadsworth, Ben Nicholson, Paul Nash, Frances Hodgkins (whose place was subsequently given over to Tristram Hillier), Edward Burra, John Bigge, and John Armstrong; and the architects Wells Coates and Colin Lucas. Cooper actually served as secretary of this short-lived but influential group — a curious fact in light of the adamant disdain he later had for English art of the twentieth century. Herbert Read edited the book *Unit One: The Modern Movement in English Architecture, Painting and Sculpture* published in 1934. The group, described by Paul Nash as representing "that thing which is recognized as peculiarly *of today* in painting, sculpture and architecture,"[10] first exhibited together at the Mayor Gallery on April 10, 1934.

The schedule of exhibitions at the Mayor Gallery during the rest of the thirties reveals the gallery's important role in the realm of contemporary art, as well as the richness of Cooper's community and his intense personal commitment to contemporary art. The gallery's program for 1934 included England's first one-person exhibition of works by Paul Klee, *20th Century Classics* (with works by Braque, Gris, Léger, and Picasso), *Paintings by Paul Guillaume*,[11] *Watercolors by George Grosz*, and a presentation of Picasso drawings of 1900 to 1934. Exhibitions in 1935 included *Some Paintings by Picasso, Gris and Léger*, *Paintings by Paul Klee*, and *Jean Cocteau Drawings*. In 1936 the gallery featured *L'Effort Moderne*, a selection of works from the collection of the French dealer Léonce Rosenberg. A decade earlier, Mayor's gallery on Sackville Street had shown Cubist works from Rosenberg's Galerie de l'Effort Moderne.[12] In 1936 the Mayor Gallery showed *Abstract Paintings by American Artists*, arranged by Albert Eugene Gallatin's Gallery of Living Art, which was then at New York University. In November of that year, the Mayor Gallery exhibition of paintings by Gris was hailed as "the first complete exhibition of his work in London." [13] A December exhibition of gouaches and small oils included works by Klee, Miró, Georges Rouault, and Graham Sutherland, among others. Works by Braque, Henri Matisse, and Picasso were included in an exhibition in February 1937. Max Ernst was featured in an exhibition in June of that year.[14] The Mayor Gallery, then, played an undeniably important role in the promotion of contemporary art in England in the thirties. The influence of the Mayor Gallery, along with that of other prominent galleries in that decade, has yet to be adequately explored.[15]

There were other important neighbors on Cork Street. From January 1938 until June 1939, Peggy Guggenheim's Guggenheim Jeune was at 30 Cork Street, and E.L.T. Mesens' London Gallery was at number 28.[16] Mesens, a Belgian Surrealist painter, promoted especially his fellow Surrealists in the London Gallery. He had been a member of the organizing committee of the *International Surrealist Exhibition* that took place at the New Burlington Galleries in 1936. Significantly, however, Cooper's one purchase from Mesens was not a Surrealist work of art, rather a major Braque oil, *Still Life with Mandola and Metronome* (fig. 4), bought in May 1936 for £125.[17] Mesens also edited the avant-garde review *The London Bulletin*, to which Cooper submitted "Rappel à l'ordre," published in July 1938. Writing under the byline Douglas Lord, Cooper gave a scathing review of the generally conservative, poetic naturalism of works in the exhibition *Cross Sections of English Painting 1938*, and also criticized the blind nationalism that he found characteristic of the supporters of this style of realism, including the art historian Anthony Blunt.[18]

Through his affiliation with the Mayor Gallery, Cooper became acquainted with the many dealers and collectors of the time, including Albert Gallatin, Paul Guillaume, and Léonce Rosenberg. The Parisian dealer Daniel-Henry Kahnweiler was a major source for the Mayor Gallery's stock and also sold to Cooper personally.[19] From 1934 to 1936, the year before his death, the important German dealer Alfred Flechtheim, either directly or through his associate Alexander Vömel in Düsseldorf, provided the Mayor Gallery with works by artists including Grosz, Maurice Vlaminck, Gris, Renoir, and Braque. The fragmentary records preserved today at the Mayor Gallery also reveal the network that Mayor maintained with other Parisian dealers besides Kahnweiler. Pierre Colle provided the material for the gallery's exhibition of works by Jean Cocteau in 1935, as well as a number of works by Picasso over the years. Mayor purchased works by Rouault both directly from the artist and from Galerie Zak. The importance of these and other dealers to the growth of Cooper's personal collection will be demonstrated later in this essay. At this time Cooper also came to know many major private collectors, including the eminent G.F. Reber.

Cooper's contacts with the artists themselves were also significant. He met or corresponded with Braque, Cocteau, Klee, Kandinsky, Léger, Miró, Picasso, and Rouault, as well as Henry Moore and the other members of Unit One. In many cases, his early contacts initiated long-standing friendships or collaborations. Indeed, Cooper occasionally purchased directly from the artists. He obtained two recent oils from Braque in 1933.[20] Cooper's purchases from Léger occured in three groups. In November 1936 he bought five works: one 1913 *Contraste de formes* for £40 and four related works (one oil and three gouaches), executed the year of purchase, for £5 each; these included Léger's *Composition* (1936, fig. 5).[21] In October 1937 he acquired four recent gouaches for £7 each.[22] And in 1939, for £5 each, Cooper bought up to seven drawings.[23]

Few records documenting Cooper's activities in the Mayor Gallery exist. While many records were destroyed during the war, some of the facts may also have been distorted after his stormy break from the gallery in 1937/38, making it difficult to disentangle Cooper's activities as director of the Mayor Gallery from those as a private collector. Cooper's records of his personal collection indicate several purchases from the Mayor Gallery. In 1938 he bought at least four works from the gallery, including, in March, a 1919 Gris still life for £50.[24] In June he bought an early Braque, *Landscape at La Ciotat* (fig. 6),[25] and in July, two Gris drawings.[26]

A particularly striking pattern, and a significant clue to the dissolution of the partnership, emerges in the Mayor Gallery ledger books. Cooper in effect violated the partnership in 1937/38 and certainly undermined the financial success of the joint venture when he withdrew numerous pictures that he had previously committed to the gallery stock. Though this is difficult to substantiate, it seems that more and more Cooper purchased for himself, shifting his money and efforts to his personal collection, and perhaps even exploiting Mayor's elaborate social and business network for the benefit of his own personal goals.

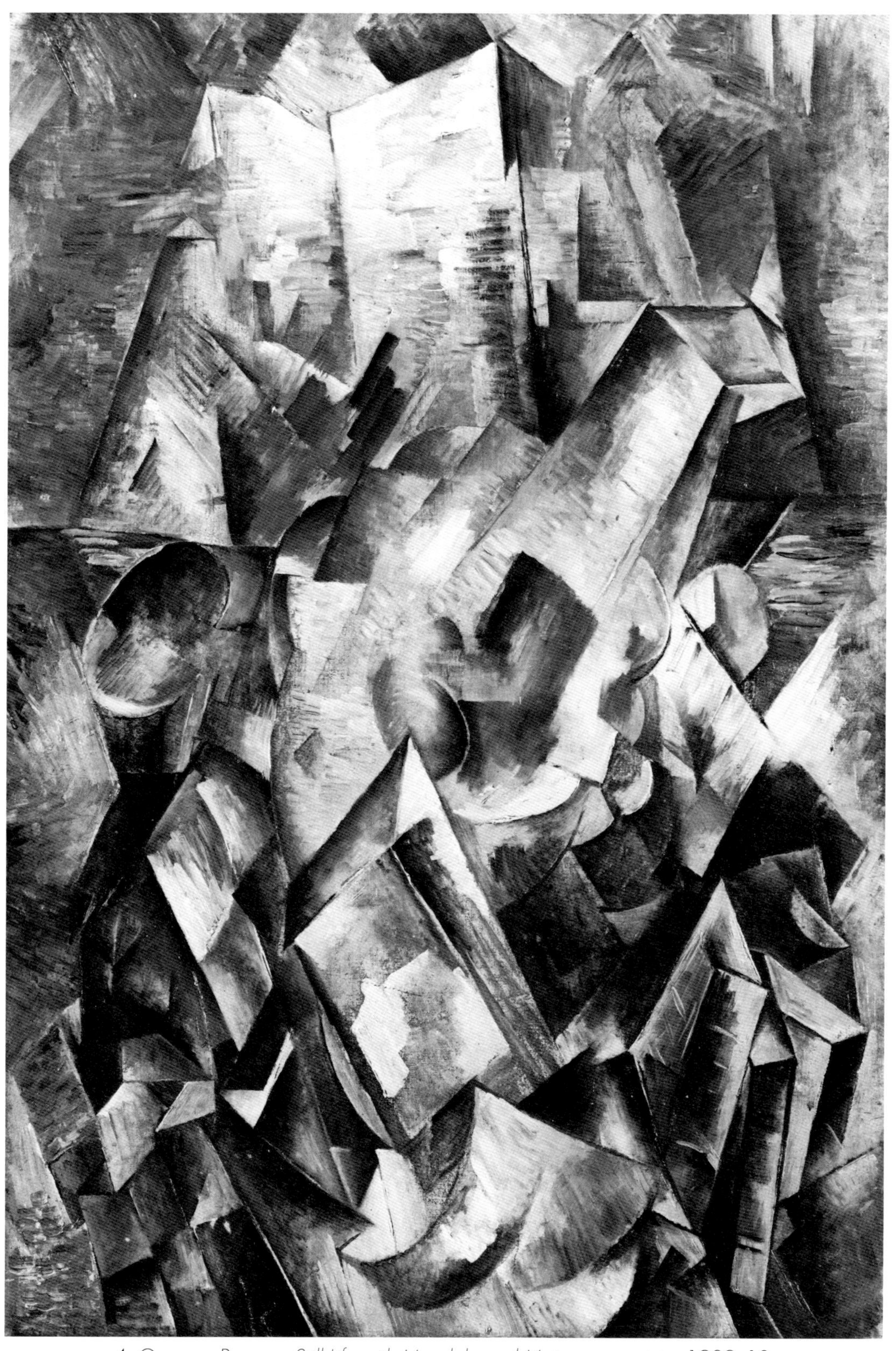

4. Georges Braque, *Still Life with Mandola and Metronome,* winter 1909–10
oil on canvas, 31⅞ × 21$^{5}/_{16}$ in. (81 × 54.2 cm.), private collection.

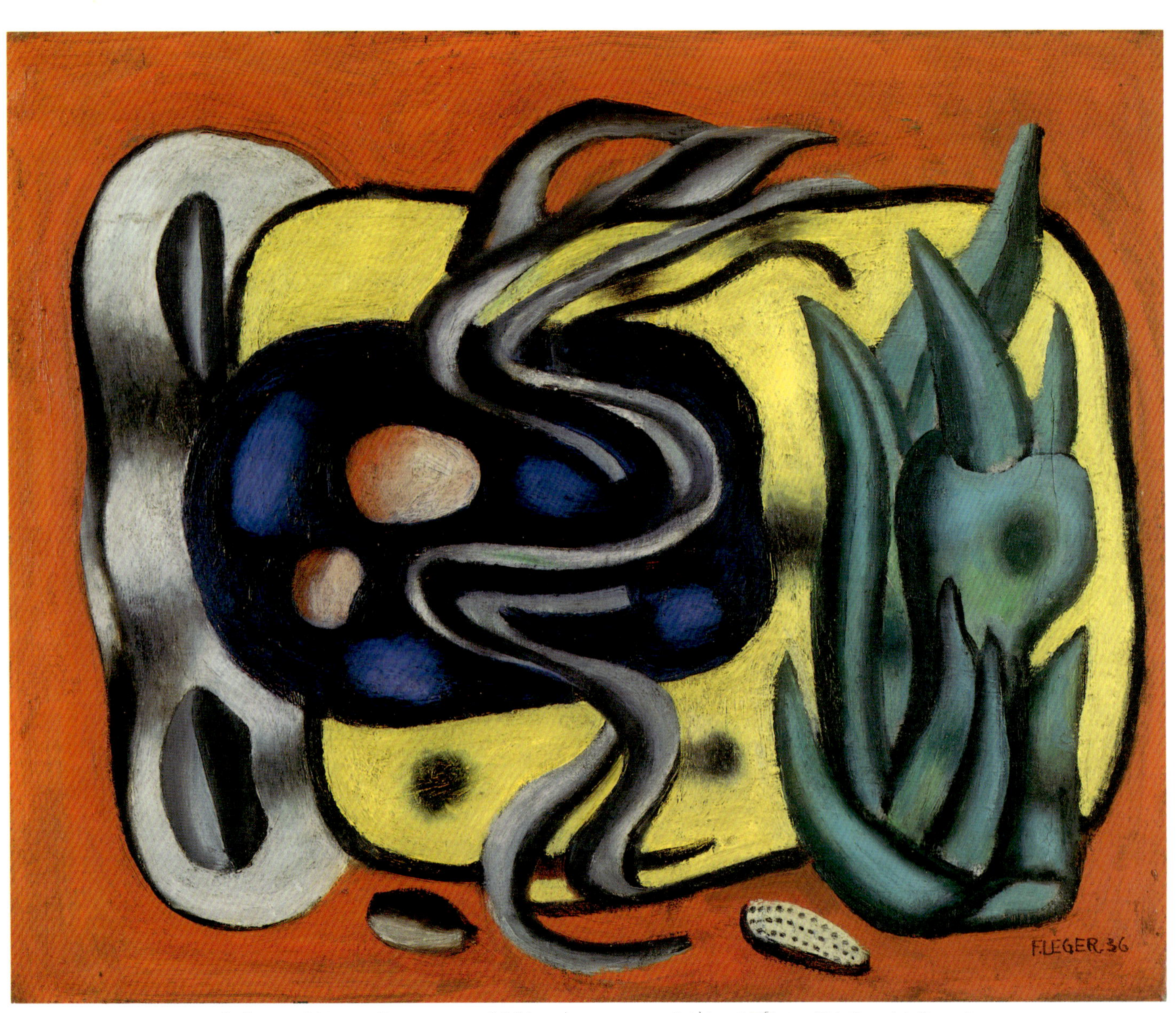

5. Fernand Léger, *Composition,* 1936, oil on canvas, 14½ × 17⅝ in. (36.8 × 44.8 cm.)
courtesy of the Fogg Art Museum, Harvard University, Cambridge, Massachusetts
gift of Mr. and Mrs. Harold Gershinowitz.

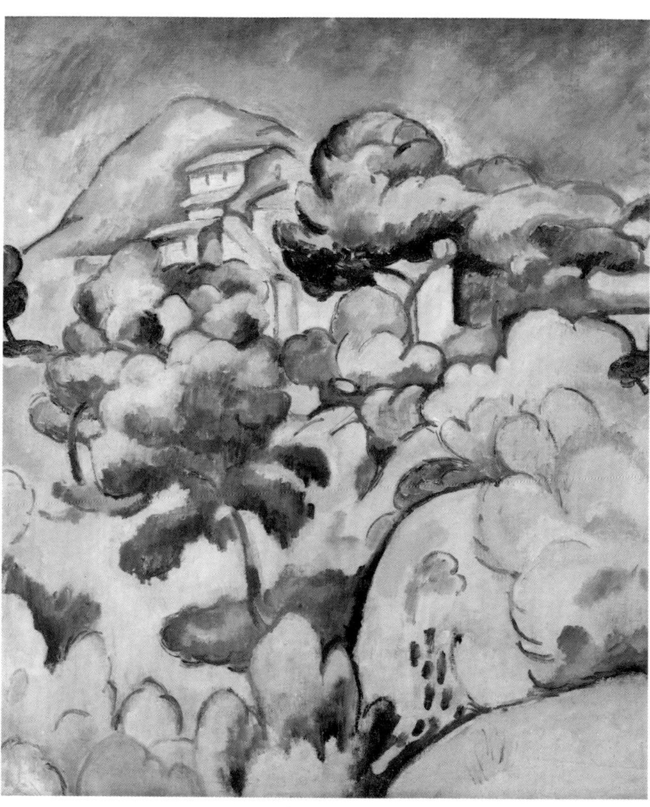

6. Georges Braque, *Landscape at La Ciotat*, 1907, oil on canvas, 28¼ x 23⅜ in. (71.8 x 59.4 cm.), The Museum of Modern Art, New York; acquired through the Katherine S. Dreier and Adele R. Levy Bequests.

DANIEL-HENRY KAHNWEILER

On the immediate level, Cooper's association with the Mayor Gallery provided him with the essential contacts for the quick and judicious purchases he made between 1933 and 1939. In a more general sense, this community of colleagues and friends helped to inform the young collector's evolving aesthetic philosophy, his dedication to Cubism, and his art criticism and scholarship.

The correspondence between Daniel-Henry Kahnweiler (1884-1976) and Cooper during this period demonstrates that the two men maintained a substantial and profound exchange of ideas. The letters may further reveal a significant impact on Cooper's emerging aesthetic understanding. Kahnweiler was long established as a champion of Cubism, and in 1920 his *Der Weg zum Kubismus* was published in Munich. Early in 1936 Alfred Flechtheim apparently notified Kahnweiler in Paris of the Mayor Gallery's plans for an exhibition to include not only works by the four great Cubist masters — Braque, Gris, Léger, and Picasso — but also works by the lesser artists in the Cubist orbit, including Albert Gleizes, Jean Metzinger, Georges Valmier, and Auguste Herbin. Kahnweiler objected vehemently to this plan, arguing that in England it was especially important to distinguish between the masters of Cubism and the hangers-on, for the appreciation of this movement was still only incipient. He felt that the inclusion of secondary figures in the movement would only obscure the quality and meaning of the true Cubists, a concept that he had expounded with great passion throughout his career. Kahnweiler threatened to bring an end to any further collaboration with the gallery. His insistence on the qualitative distinction of the four major Cubist artists may well have had an enduring impact on Cooper's understanding of Cubism, providing the foundation for Cooper's often-repeated insistence on the "essential" or "true" Cubism.[27] In response to one of Cooper's letters, Kahnweiler also apparently expressed strong criticism of a proposed magazine to be devoted exclusively to abstract art. This revealed Kahnweiler's own prejudices against pure abstraction, which may have informed Cooper's lifelong lack of sympathy for abstract art.

Kahnweiler not only provided guidance for the conceptual basis of Cooper's collection, but was also Cooper's direct source for a number of important works. In November 1936 Cooper purchased three works by Gris (for £35, £175, and £80)[28] and an important *Contraste de formes* by Léger (£10, fig. 7).[29] In June 1937 he purchased *Harlequin* by Juan Gris (£100) and acquired another still life by exchange.[30] He also bought a 1914 Picasso, *Still Life with Peaches and Playing Cards*, in 1937 for £22.[31] In November 1938 he purchased, for £1 each, three early drawings of nudes by Léger. These included Léger's *Standing*

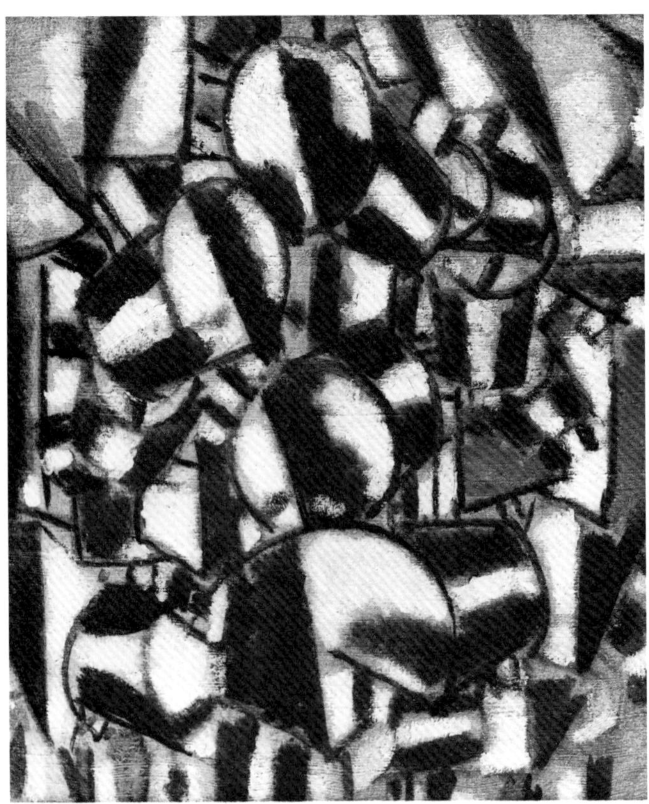

7. Fernand Léger, *Contraste de formes,* 1913, oil on canvas, 21⅜ × 18⅛ in. (55 × 46 cm.), private collection.

Nude (1911) and his *Male Nude Seen from Behind* (fig. 8).[32]

In addition to his direct influence on Cooper, Kahnweiler evidently played an important commercial role in the Mayor Gallery, providing works of art and partaking in the sales commissions. This arrangement also involved his colleague and business partner, Alfred Flechtheim.

ALFRED FLECHTHEIM

Alfred Flechtheim (1878-1937) and Kahnweiler had been friends since 1909 or 1910. Kahnweiler had inspired and encouraged Flechtheim's shift from trading in grain to dealing in contemporary (and especially French) art. Kahnweiler's brother Gustav had worked with Flechtheim in his gallery in Berlin from 1921, and had directed Flechtheim's branch gallery in Frankfurt beginning the following year.

Hitler's gradual consolidation of power, coupled with the continued effects of the world economic crisis, forced Flechtheim to close his galleries in Düsseldorf and Berlin in November 1933, and to move first to Paris, then to London. Kahnweiler and Mayor seem to have shared reponsibility for expediting Flechtheim's safe exit from Germany, and more specifically, were instrumental in establishing his activities with the Mayor Gallery toward the end of 1933. Flechtheim continued, however, to travel back to Germany until the autumn of 1934, when it finally became too dangerous. It appears that much of his gallery stock and many items from his important personal collection were sent either to the Mayor Gallery in London or to Kahnweiler's Galerie Simon in Paris. The fact that Flechtheim's gallery records and personal library (unfortunately destroyed during the war) were left with Fred Mayor upon his death attests to the friendship between the two men. Flechtheim's involvement with the Mayor Gallery seems to have been his most attractive alternative after a hoped-for position as manager of Paul Rosenberg's gallery in New York failed to materialize.

Flechtheim played a central role in the Mayor Gallery. It was he who was the instrumental force in organizing such groundbreaking exhibitions as those in 1934 of Klee, of *20th Century Classics*, of George Grosz, of Braque, and of Picasso, as well as a Marie Laurencin exhibition in December. The gallery began 1935 with a *Picasso, Gris, Léger* exhibition in February. During February and March the Mayor Gallery exhibited twenty-four works by Elie Lascaux from the Galerie Simon.

The collaboration with the Mayor Gallery evidently could not prove lucrative for either Flechtheim or Kahnweiler. Kahnweiler had clearly hoped that this London venture might offer some relief to the Continental art market, considerably tightened since the economic crash in 1930. For Flechtheim, in exile from his native Germany and having left behind the galler-

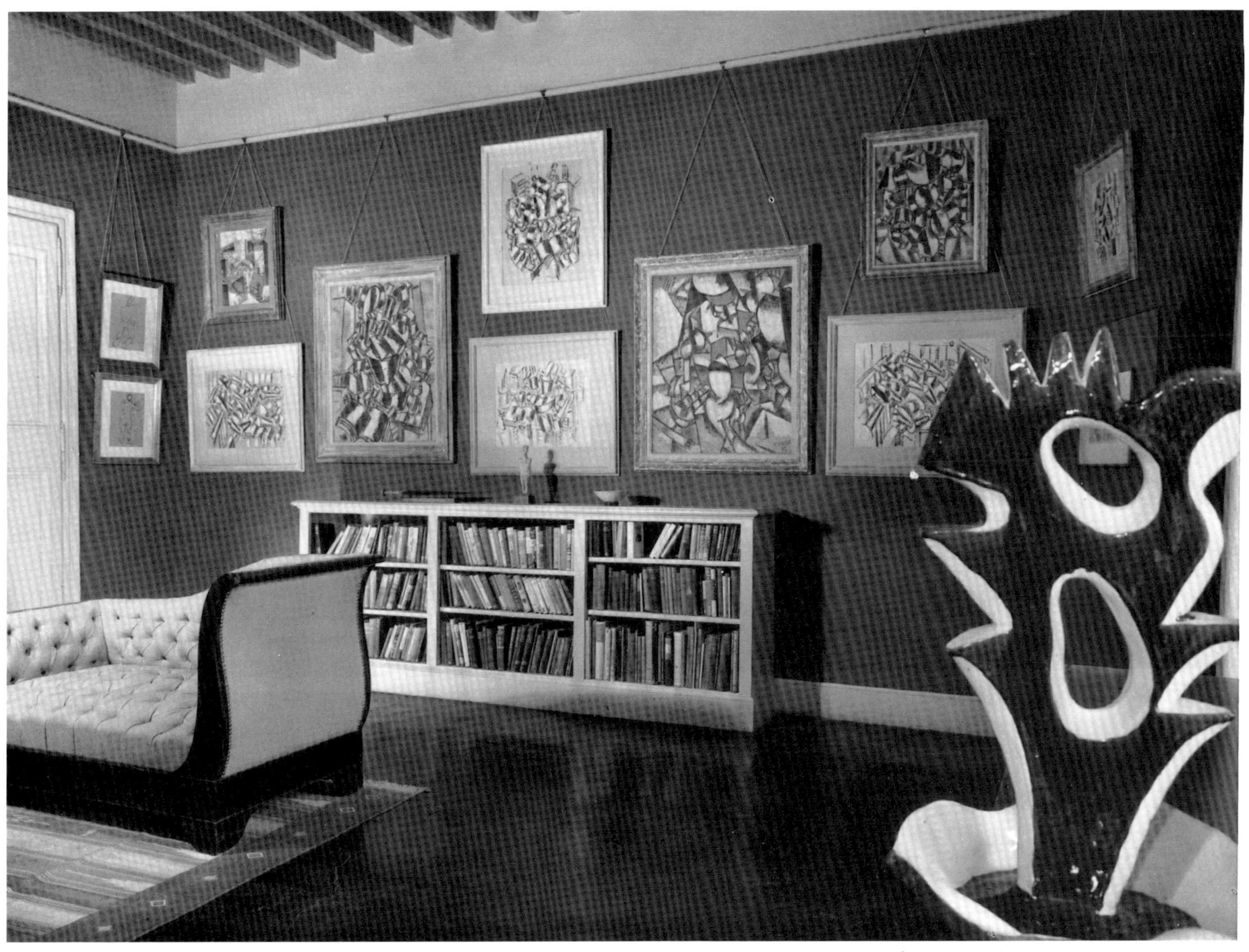

8. The interior of Cooper's Château de Castille, c. 1955, with works by Léger from his collection. Left to right at top: *Male Nude Seen from Behind,* 1911, ink on paper; *View of Paris,* 1912, oil on canvas; *Still Life on a Table,* 1914, gouache on paper; *Contraste de formes,* 1913, oil on canvas; and *The Mason,* 1918, watercolor on paper. Left to right at bottom: *Standing Nude,* 1911, ink on paper; *Two Women Reclining,* 1913, gouache on paper; *Still Life with a Book,* 1914, oil on canvas; *Nature Morte,* 1913, gouache and oil on paper; *Landscape,* 1913, oil on millboard; *Two Reclining Women,* 1913, gouache on paper; obscured at far right, Study for *Curtain for La Création du monde,* 1922, pencil on paper; and in right foreground, *Fleur* or *Red Cock,* 1940s, glazed ceramic. (Photo, Robert Doisneau.)

ies that he had built up since 1913, first in Düsseldorf, then in Berlin, Frankfurt, and Cologne, the enterprise was a question of sheer survival. For Kahnweiler, the Picasso exhibition in autumn 1934, for instance, was a test of the viability of the London market. The quandary was, how low could one allow the prices to fall in order to attract potential buyers? By December of 1935 Kahnweiler wanted out of his arrangement for commissions with Flechtheim and the Mayor Gallery. The following year, Flechtheim complained bitterly about the lack of response to *Picasso, Gris, Léger*, describing how he and his colleagues were victims of a misguided support of Cubism. It was with this financial desperation and moral disillusionment that Flechtheim began to collaborate with Geoffrey Agnew from the Leicester Gallery. Despite his professed withdrawal from Cubism, Flechtheim organized an exhibition of Léger and Togores at Leicester's. Yet he also seemed to turn his energies to nineteenth-century art, organizing, for example, an exhibition of works by Degas for Thomas Agnew & Sons, Ltd. In October his *Exhibition of Masters of French 19th Century Painting* at the New Burlington Galleries was hailed as a great success. One of his final projects was *Seurat and his Friends*, also for Agnew's. Flechtheim died on March 9, 1937 from blood poisoning, the result of a minor injury.[33]

Cooper's contact with Flechtheim was significant not merely for the handful of important works that Cooper purchased for his private collection, but also for Flechtheim's passionate relationship to contemporary French and modern German art, and for his influential position within the tightly knit international cabal of powerful dealers and collectors (fig. 9).

Flechtheim was indeed an important source for Cooper's private collection. The handwritten notecard records of Cooper's collection indicate at least seven acquisitions in 1934 and 1935 from Alfred Flechtheim, including four works by Picasso and one work each by Gris, Klee, and Léger. The works by Picasso included *Still Life with Dead Birds* (1912), bought in 1935 for £150 (fig. 10);[34] *The Soldier* (c. 1901), purchased in 1934 for £5 (fig. 11);[35] *Ex Libris Guillaume Apollinaire* (1905), a gift from Flechtheim;[36] and *Head of a Woman* (1909), purchased in 1934 for £20.[37] The Gris was *Fruit Dish and Guitar* (1925), purchased for £3.[38]

Cooper had an ongoing interest in the work of Paul Klee that we might attribute to Flechtheim's influence. Flechtheim had championed Klee, exhibiting his works repeatedly in his galleries. His stock evidently formed the core of the Mayor Gallery's monographic exhibition of Klee's pictures in January 1934.[39] Cooper purchased Klee's *Barockbildnis* from Flechtheim for £20; this gouache had been included in the *20th Century Classics* exhibition at the Mayor Gallery in February 1934.[40] Between that exhibition and another one-person show in May 1935, Cooper and Klee corresponded with each other, and the letters often included an indirect exchange of greetings between Klee and his long-time supporter, Flechtheim.[41] Cooper's enthusiasm is made evident by the approximately eighteen works by Klee that he eventually came to own (see below, page 45), as well as by the publication of his monograph on the artist in 1949.

The Léger that Cooper obtained from Flechtheim in 1934, *Man and Dog in a Landscape* (1921), was apparently a gift and was returned to Kahnweiler under interesting circumstances: in Cooper's notecard for this painting he remarked, "This picture apparently belonged to Kahnweiler and A.F. had no rights over it. In November 1937 I returned it to Kahnweiler."[42] This confusion concerning the work's ownership indicates the complex business arrangements between Kahnweiler and Flechtheim, the connections between those two dealers and the Mayor Gallery, and, finally, the ambiguous relationship between the Mayor Gallery and Cooper himself.[43]

THE GROWTH OF COOPER'S COLLECTION 1933 to 1935

An overview of Cooper's purchases during these years reveals that they began relatively quietly in 1933 and 1934, but were to accelerate dramatically from 1935 until late 1939, when his collecting was eclipsed by the war. The year 1933 was indeed a rather gentle

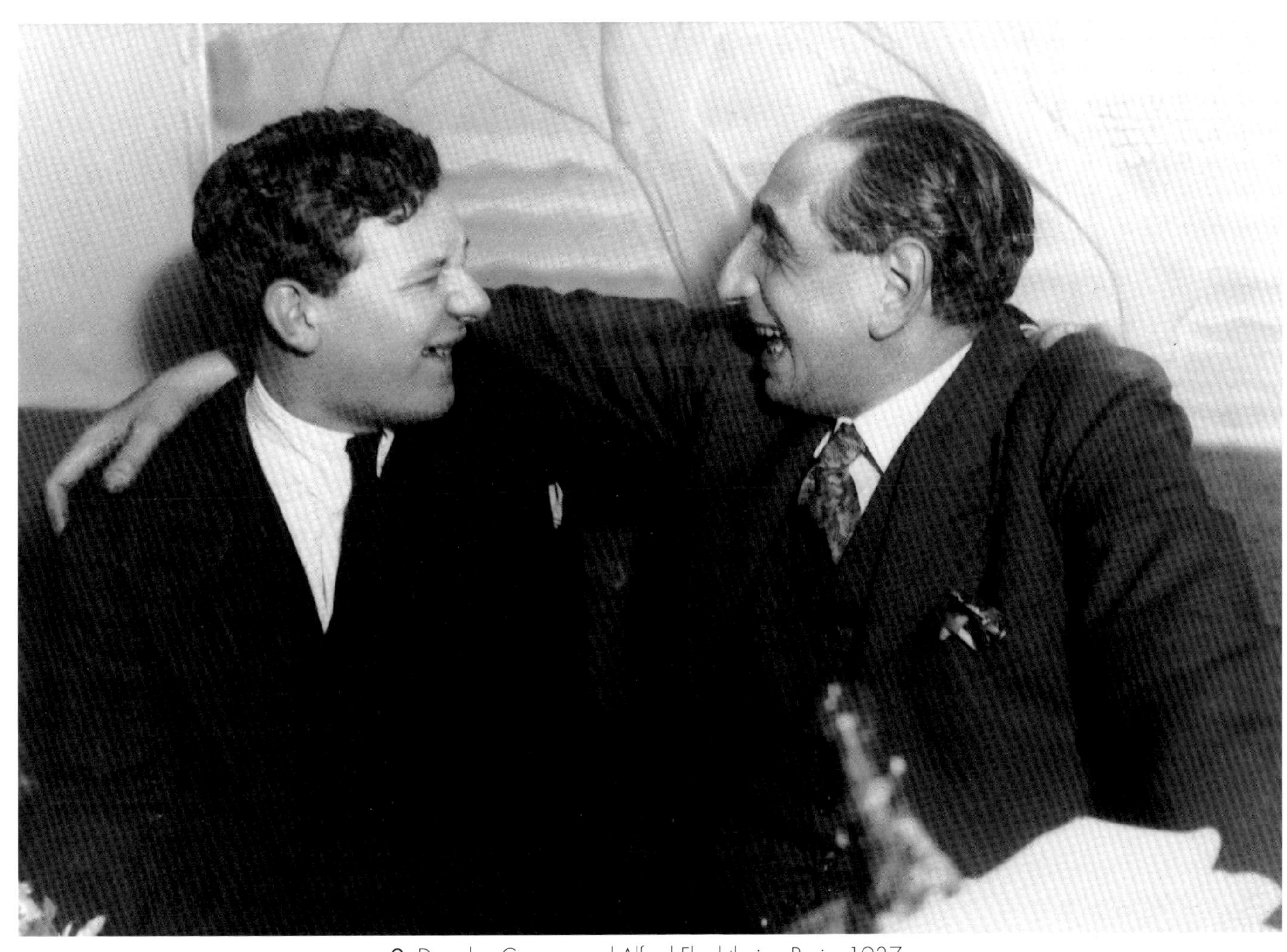

9. Douglas Cooper and Alfred Flechtheim, Paris, 1937.

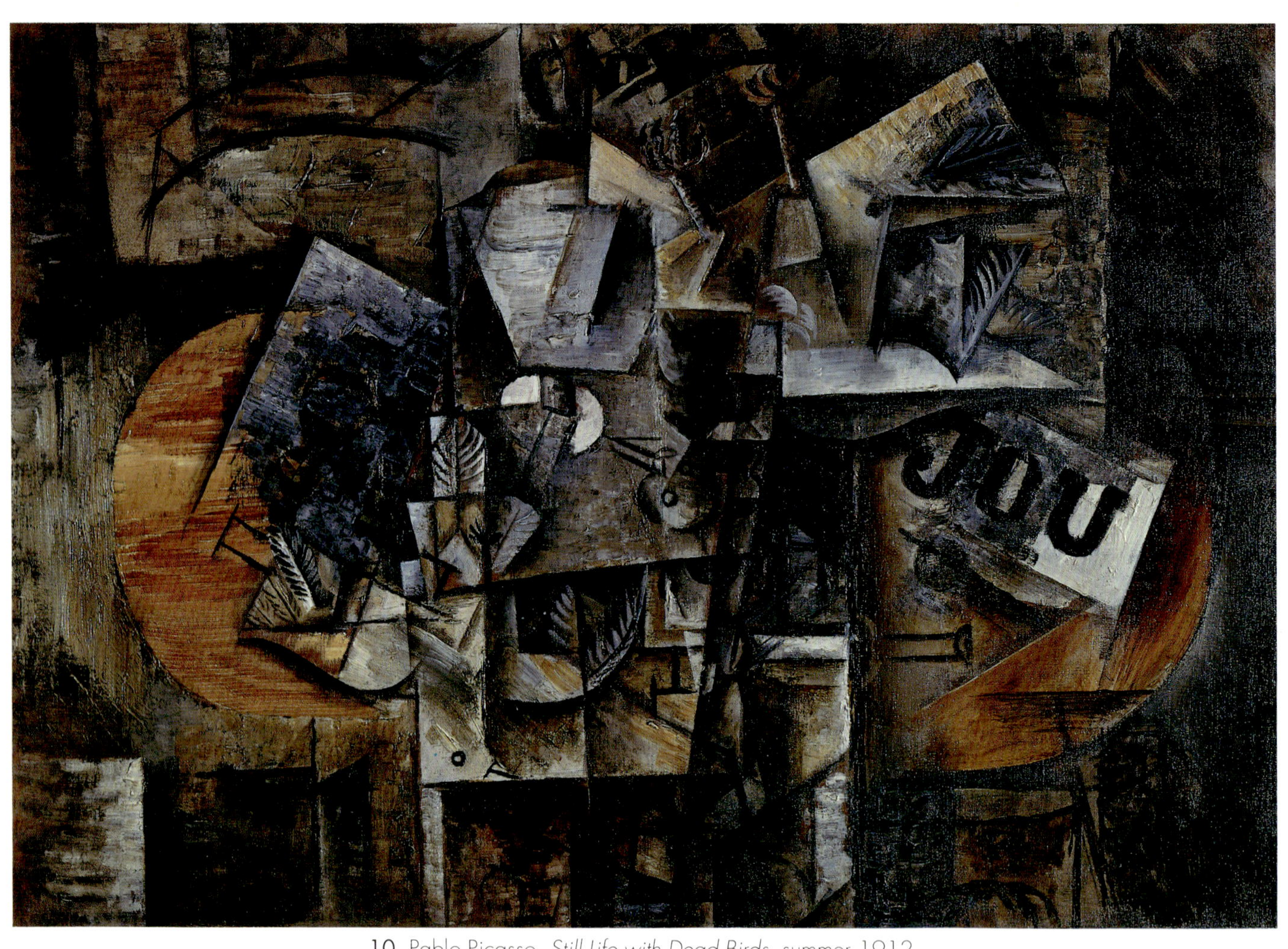

10. Pablo Picasso, *Still Life with Dead Birds,* summer 1912
oil on canvas, 18⅛ × 25⅝ in. (46 × 65 cm.), Museo del Prado, Madrid.

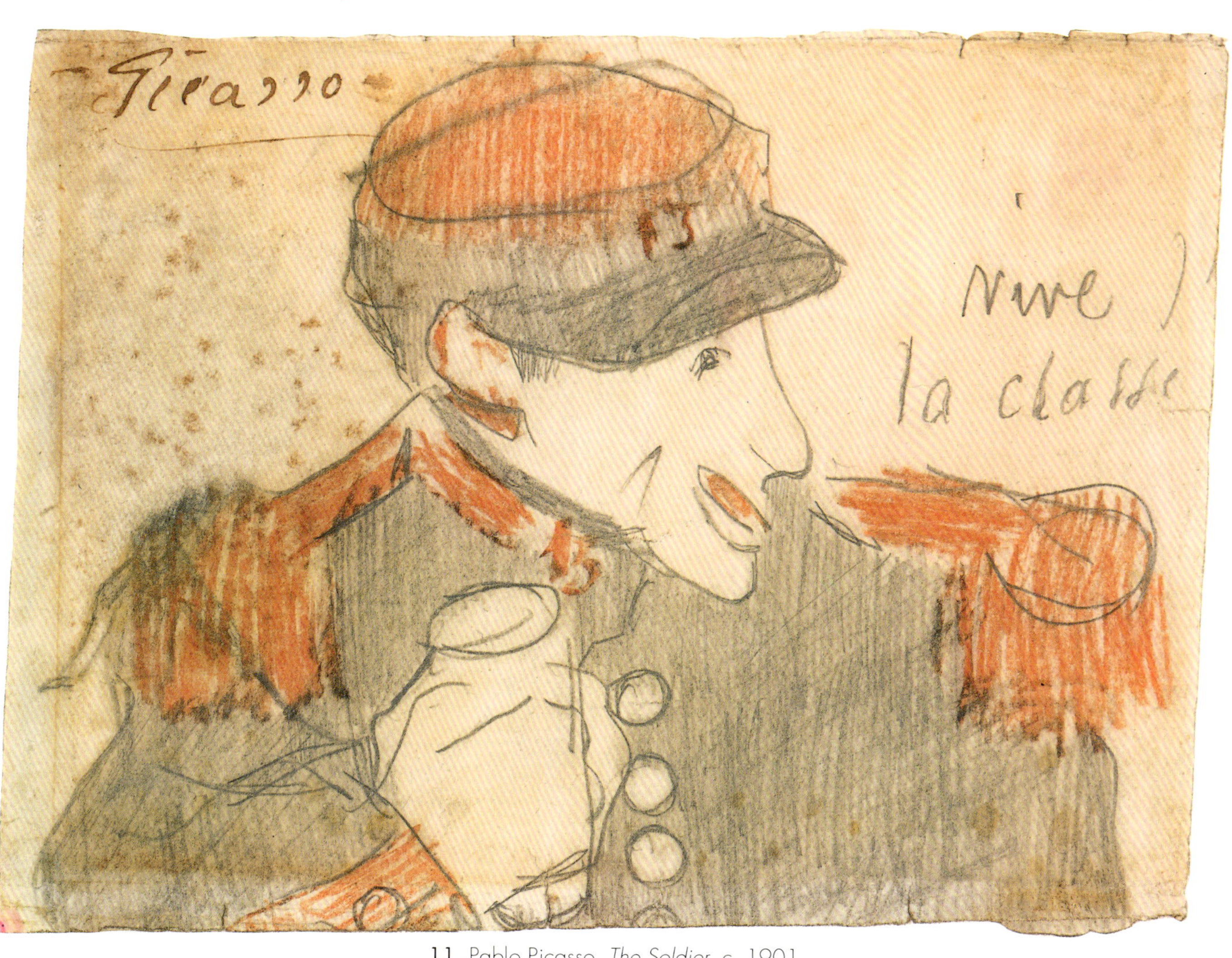

11. Pablo Picasso, *The Soldier*, c. 1901
crayon on paper, 6 × 4¼ in. (15.2 × 10.8 cm.), private collection.

beginning, because Cooper appears to have acquired only four works of art. These included a small self-portrait by Cocteau, given to him by the artist in May of that year; a small drawing by Henry Moore purchased from the artist for £7; his first Picasso, *Head of a Woman, Casket and Apple*, purchased from the balletomane Arnold Haskell for £8;[44] and, curiously, an oil by Cézanne, *La Préparation du banquet* (c. 1890) bought from Pierre Loeb for £900.[45]

In 1934, in addition to the four works purchased from Alfred Flechtheim mentioned above, Cooper obtained two gouaches by Joan Miró, an engraving by Stanley William Hayter, and a gouache given to him by Fernand Léger, testimony to the growing friendship between the young collector and Léger.[46] The engraving by Hayter was a gift from the artist as well, though it is unclear as to whether Cooper had any special friendship with this British painter, printmaker, and founder of the noted print workshops Atelier 17.[47] Cooper's first purchase of a Miró, a 1933 gouache bought in 1934 for £10, is an early indication of his sustained interest in that Spaniard's work.[48] Later in the year, Miró presented Cooper with a maquette for the *Programme, Ballets russes de Monte-Carlo, New York, 1933-34*.[49]

In 1935 Cooper began to collect in earnest. As noted already above, his three purchases from Flechtheim included Picasso's major *Still Life with Dead Birds* of 1912 (fig. 10). He purchased, as well, two Picasso still lifes dated 1920 from André Level of the Galerie Percier (£10 and £12).[50] In February he traded his Cézanne, purchased two years earlier, to Paul Rosenberg for another major Picasso oil, *Still Life with Fruit Dish and Mandolin* (1932, fig. 12).[51] This major acquisition of a Picasso from just three years earlier, along with the various works by Léger, Miró, and others dating from the 1930s, demonstrates Cooper's commitment to contemporary art.

LÉONCE ROSENBERG

In 1935 Cooper initiated an intense business relationship with Léonce Rosenberg (1877-1947) when he bought his first Léger from the dealer. By the end of 1937, Cooper had bought at least another nine works by Léger from Rosenberg. As we recall, in 1936 sixteen works from Rosenberg's collection and gallery had been exhibited in *L'Effort Moderne*, which opened at the Mayor Gallery on April 16.[52] In 1935 Cooper bought Léger's oil *Still Life with a Book* (1914), which, at £30, was by far his most expensive purchase from Rosenberg (fig. 8).[53] This was followed by the purchase of five important Léger works on paper at £4 each in January 1936. Two of these were versions of *Two Reclining Women* (fig. 13).[54] The remaining three were his study for *Woman in Red and Green* (fig. 14), his *Still Life*, and his study for *Le Balcon*.[55] Four more purchases followed in December 1937: two drawings from 1916-17 that were studies for *The Cardplayers* (£4 each); the watercolor *Composition: Man in a Factory* (1920, £7); and the oil *Still Life with Bust* (1924, £15, fig. 15).[56]

PRIVATE COLLECTORS

Zoubaloff Auction

A major source of art for Cooper during these years was the wealth of important material from private collections, sold either at auction or through direct sale. For example, the auction of part of the famous collection of the composer, painter, and collector Jacques Zoubaloff (1876-1941) late in 1935 at the Hôtel Drouot in Paris created a stir in the international art world.[57] Zoubaloff had already made important gifts to French museums, including works by Antoine-Louis Barye, Camille Corot, Théodore Chassériau, Henri Regnault, Honoré Daumier, François Rude, Jules Dalou, Félix Ziem, Henri Harpignies, and Jacques-Louis David. Against the background of Zoubaloff's earlier bequests and gifts to the national museums, the dispersal of his Impressionist and modern pictures seems surely to have been necessitated by financial crisis. In his introduction to the Hôtel Drouot catalogue for the 1935 sale, Guillaume Janneau, the important apologist of Cubism, lamented the lost opportunity for these modern pictures to enter a national

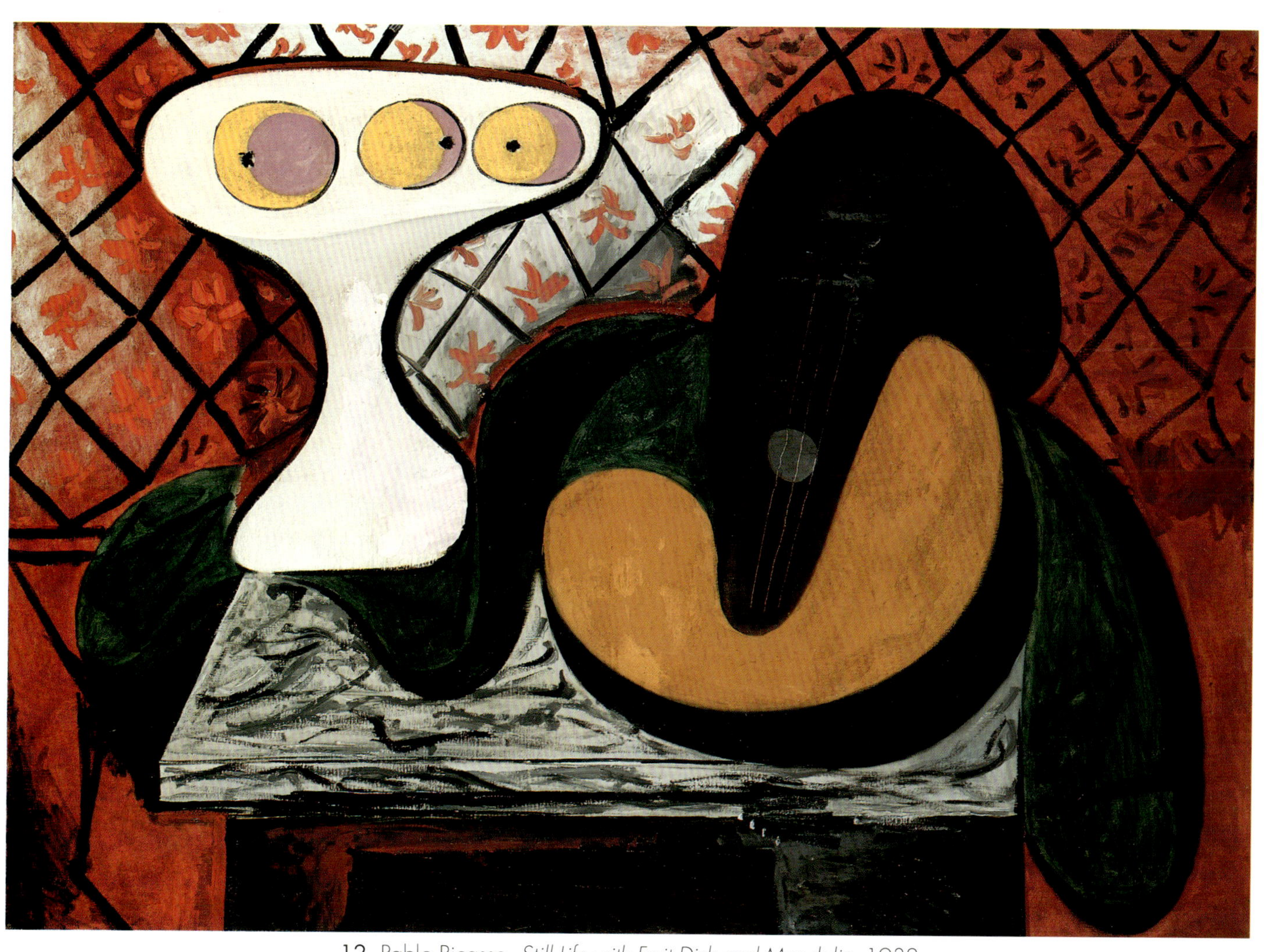

12. Pablo Picasso, *Still Life with Fruit Dish and Mandolin,* 1932
oil on canvas, 38¼ × 51$\frac{3}{16}$ in. (96.8 × 129.9 cm.), private collection.

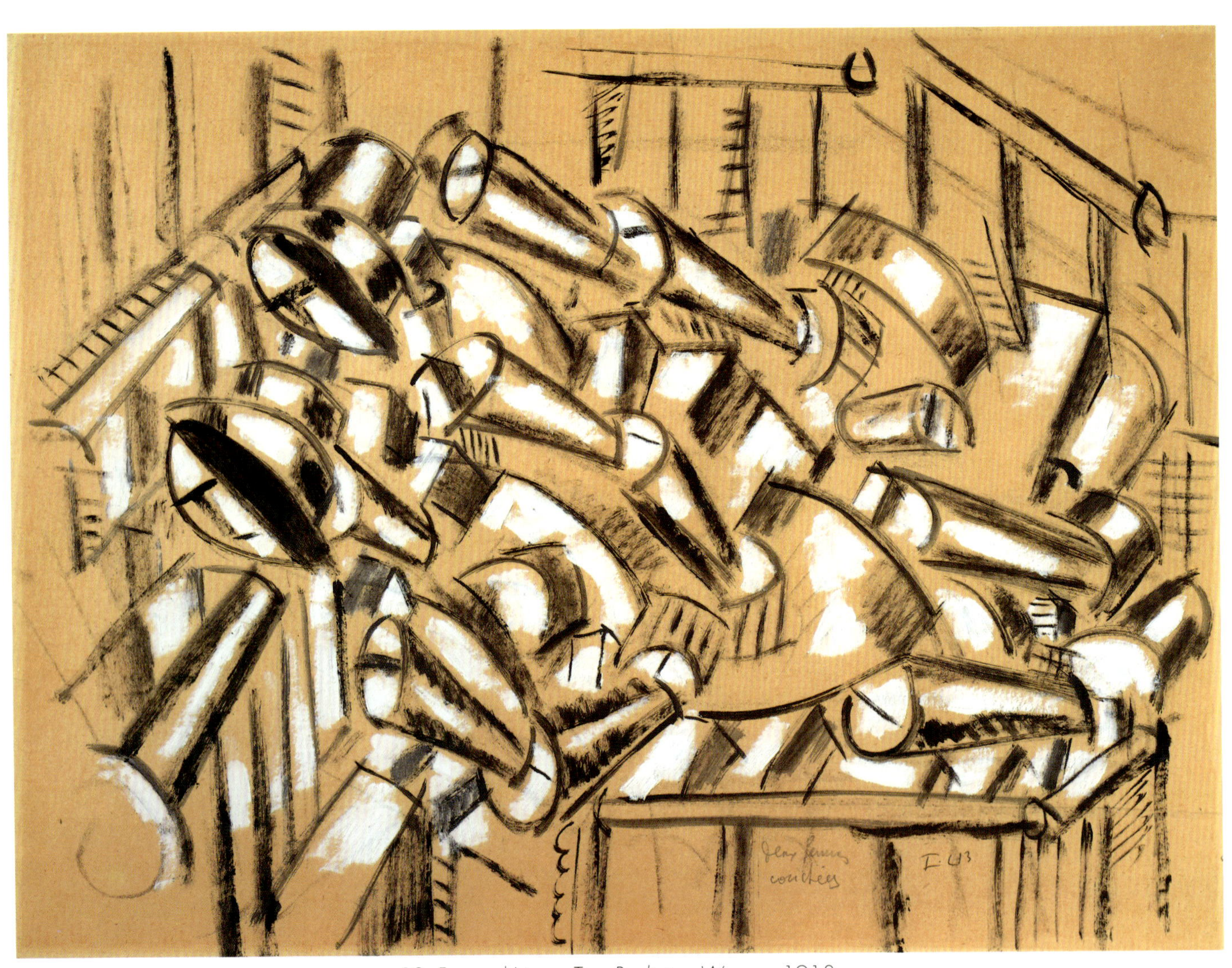

13. Fernand Léger, *Two Reclining Women,* 1913
gouache and wash on paper, 19¾ × 25⅝ in. (50.2 × 65.1 cm.)
The Metropolitan Museum of Art, New York
gift of Mr. and Mrs. William R. Acquavella, 1986.396.1.

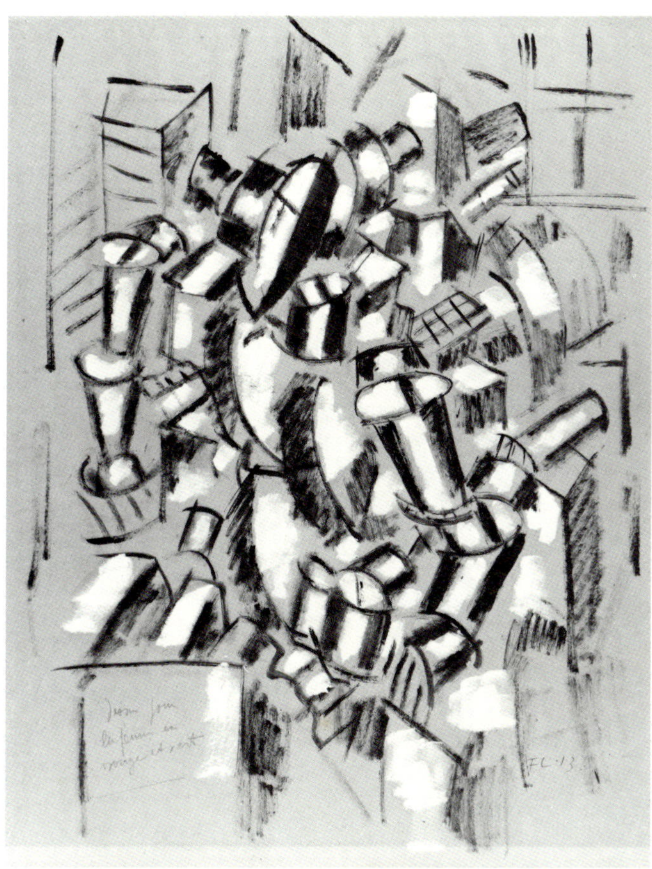

14. Fernand Léger, Study for *Woman in Red and Green,* 1913, gouache and ink on paper, 25⅝ × 19⅝ in. (65 × 50 cm.), Musée National d'Art Moderne, Centre Georges Pompidou, Paris.

museum as a coherent group. The friendship between Zoubaloff and Janneau is clear by Janneau's dedication to Zoubaloff of his 1929 book, *L'Art cubiste*: "à M. J. Z ... Hommage affectueux, G.J." Janneau may well have played a role in the formation of Zoubaloff's collection.

The sale included 206 items, including graphics, works on paper, oil paintings, and sculptures. It offered works not only by the Paris Cubists, but also by Joseph Czaky, Gino Severini, André Masson, and others.[58] Successful bidders included the Petit Palais, the Jeu de Paume, the Musée de Luxembourg, Madame Friedrich, Monsieur Crotti, and Monsieur Cuttoli. However, Douglas Cooper, who bought seven works, was one of the major purchasers. He bought three oils: Léger's *Man with Dog in a Landscape* (fig. 16),[59] Gris's *Seated Harlequin with Guitar* (fig. 17),[60] and a Picasso still life.[61] He also purchased four works on paper, all by Gris: *Harlequin with a Guitar; Still Life with Guitar, Book, and Newspaper*; a drawing for *Seated Harlequin with Guitar* (fig. 18); and *Still Life with Cup and Glass*.[62] Cooper spent a total of Fr. 14,610, or approximately £220. The sale of Zoubaloff's collection, making available a concentration of fine modern pictures, was an event from which Cooper did not fail to profit.

Pertuisot Auction

Another important auction sale took place at Christie's London in 1937. The sale held on April 23, 1937 included a group of works from the collection of Mademoiselle Pertuisot.[63] Cooper's purchases included two major works by Juan Gris, including £165 for the 1916 *Portrait of Josette Gris* now in the Prado (fig. 19), and one each by Picasso and Miró.[64] The records of this sale are interesting in two regards: first, besides Cooper, many of the active participants were also British.[65] Secondly, Cooper's purchases were recorded as "Mayor," indicating either that Cooper was present as director of the Mayor Gallery or that the works in question were purchased by Freddy Mayor, but later absorbed into Cooper's private collection. Either situation would reflect once again the intricacies of the Gallery's structure.

Earl Horter

Cooper's personal contacts with other important collectors and the purchases he made directly from them were significant to the growth of his collection during the thirties. The Philadelphian Earl Horter (1881-1940), a teacher and patron of the arts as well as a painter and printmaker, had assembled a small but concentrated collection of works by Picasso, Gris, Braque, Matisse, and Marcel Duchamp.[66] Cooper had apparently attempted to visit Horter in Philadelphia, most likely during a trip to see the newly installed Arensberg collection and the exhibition in 1936 that included some of Horter's works. Horter's correspon-

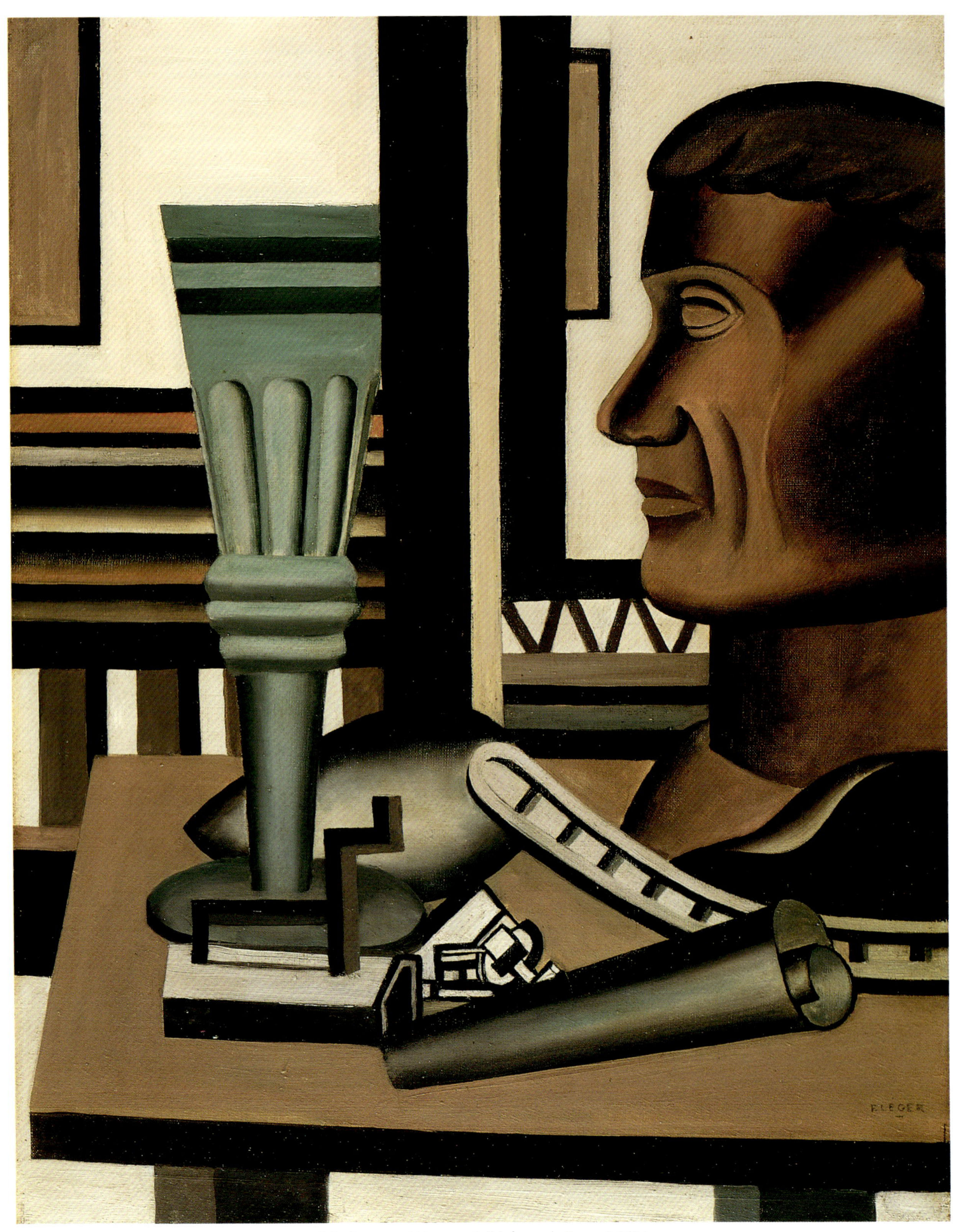

15. Fernand Léger, *Still Life with Bust,* 1924
oil on canvas, 25½ × 19¾ in. (64.6 × 49.7 cm.), private collection.

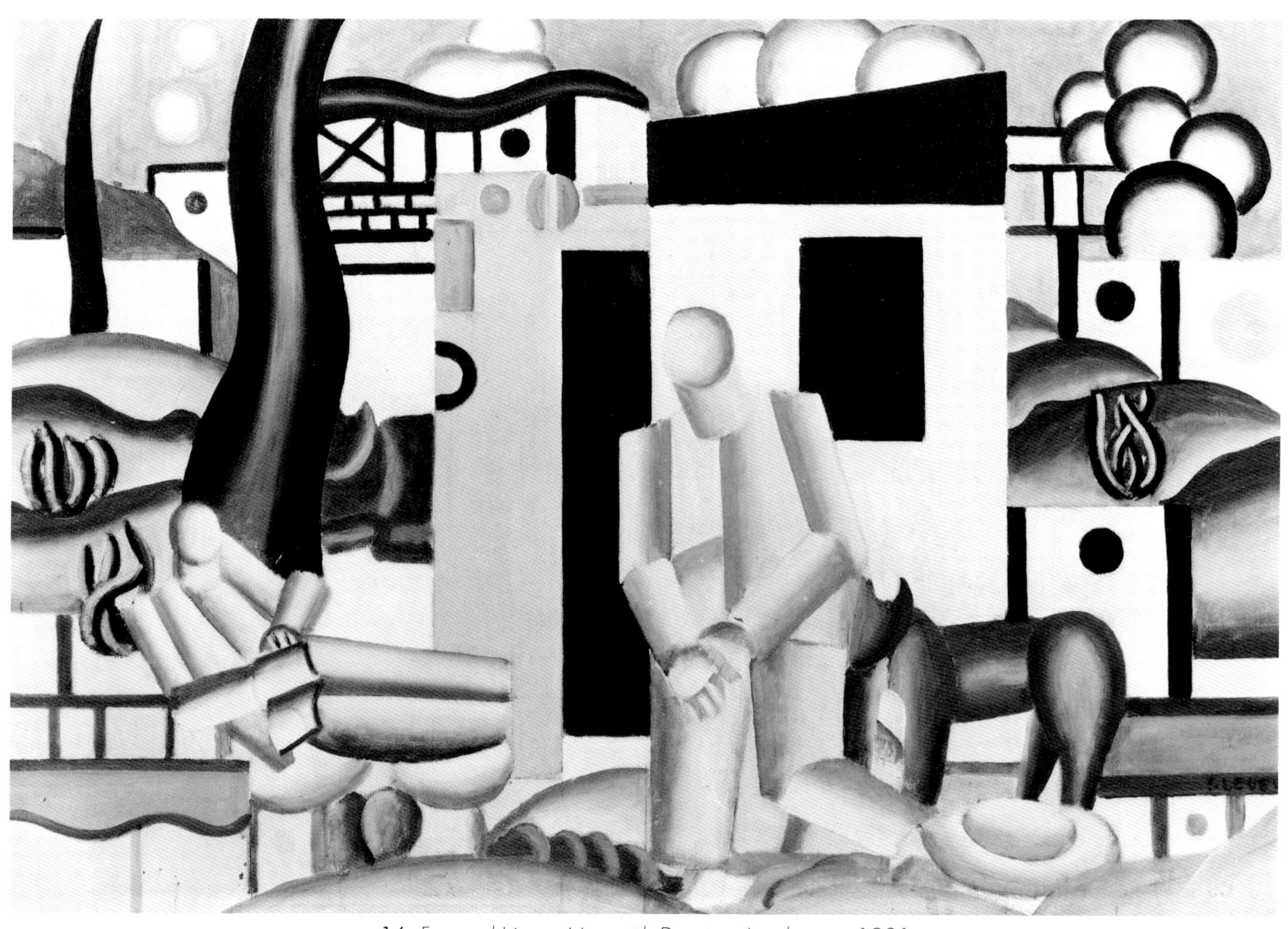

16. Fernand Léger, *Man with Dog in a Landscape,* 1921
oil on canvas, 25½ × 36 in. (64.8 × 91.4 cm.), private collection, New York.

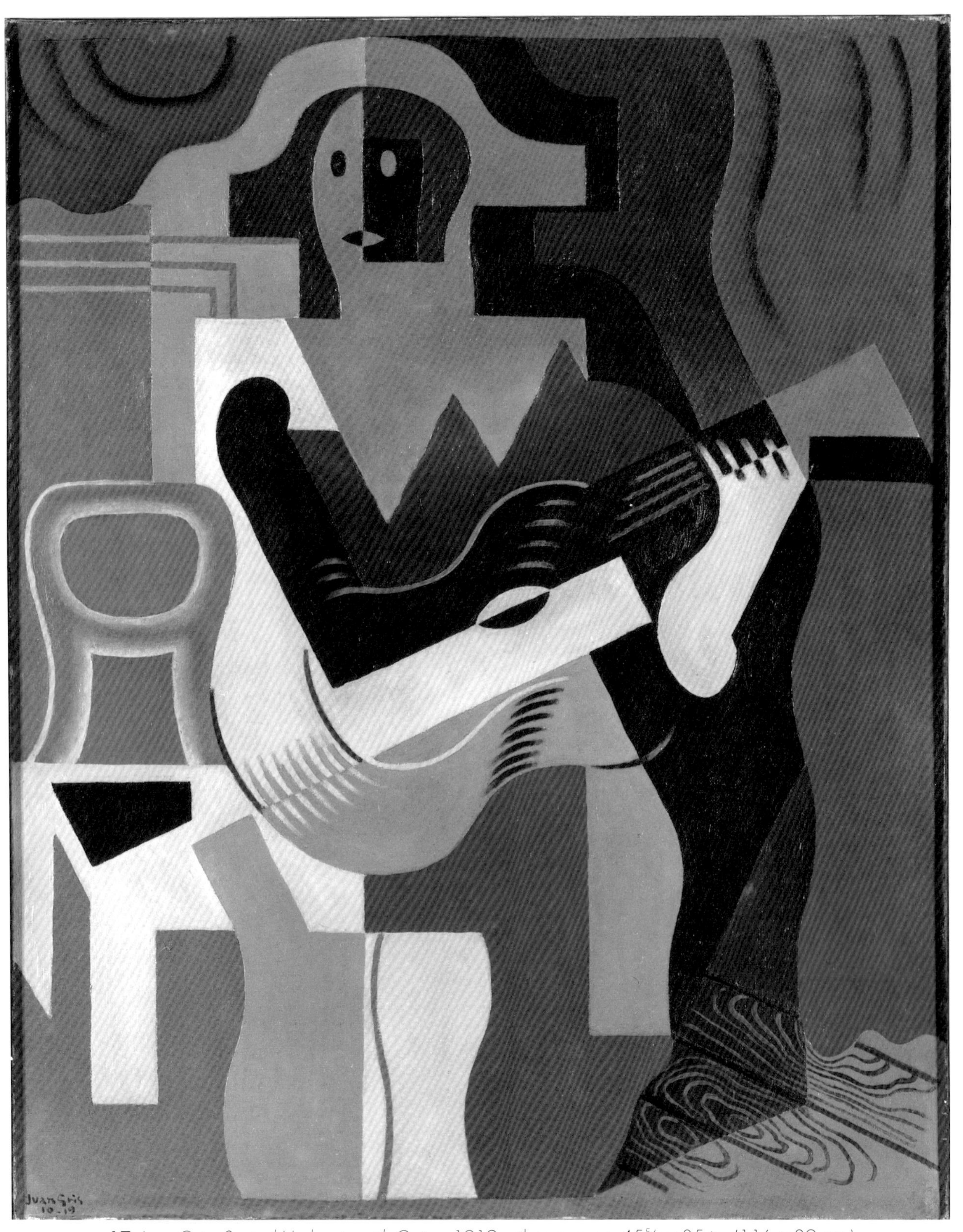

17. Juan Gris, *Seated Harlequin with Guitar*, 1919, oil on canvas, 45⅝ × 35 in. (116 × 89 cm.) Musée National d'Art Moderne, Centre Georges Pompidou, Paris.

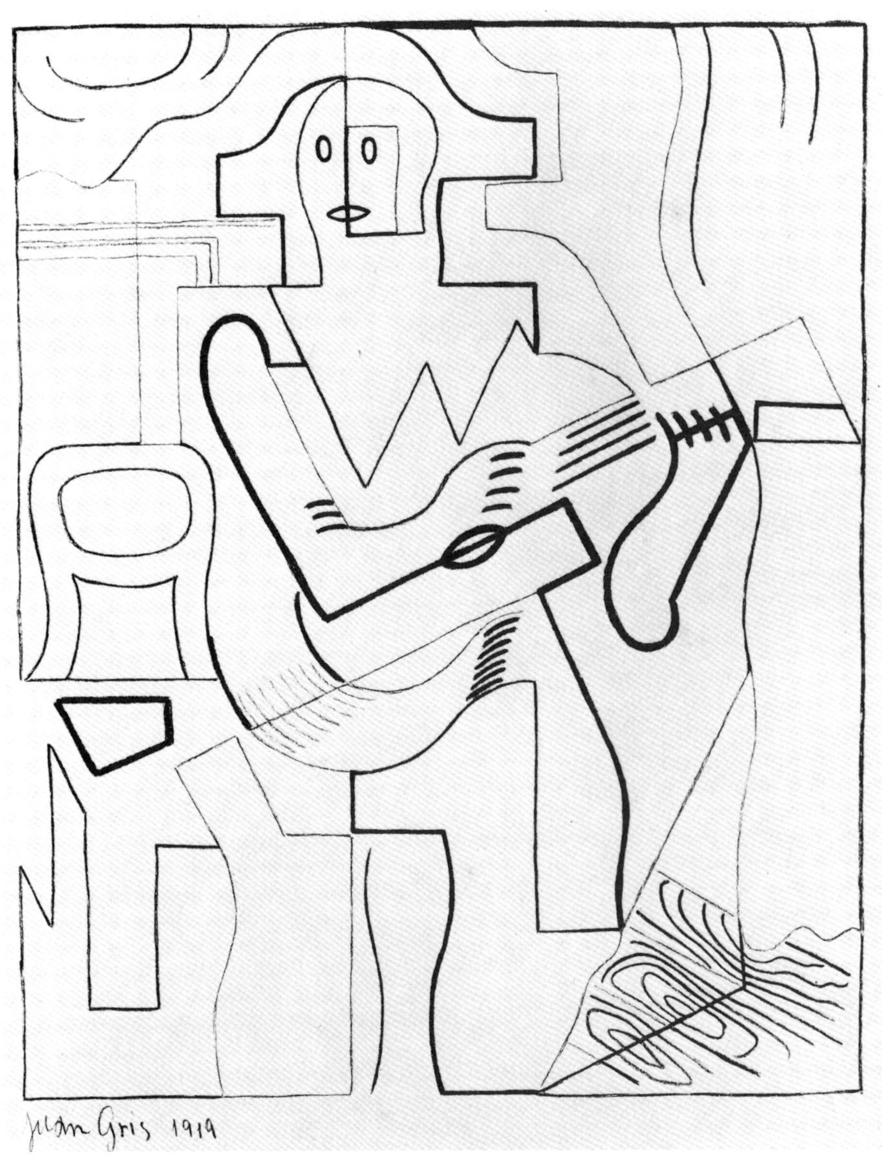

18. Juan Gris, Drawing for *Seated Harlequin with Guitar,* 1919
13¼ × 9$\frac{15}{16}$ in. (33.8 × 25.2 cm.), Galerie Louise Leiris, Paris.

dence with Cooper from 1937 clearly expresses a melancholy resignation about the financial need that necessitated the sale of the pictures he so keenly appreciated. Horter wrote

> *Sorry I did not see you when in Philadelphia, — I'm always interested in abstract painting — and in meeting anyone that is collecting same. I once had a marvellous collection but the depression... I had hoped to keep my collection — instead — but the pressure of need is always upon me lately so a sale of these would help me a lot.*[67]

In another letter he explained: "though a month ago I'd decided not to sell any more pictures — but I just found a fine Indian collection I want and need money."[68] In yet another letter, Horter agreed to a sale of at least two of his pictures, and at Cooper's request he arranged for their transport to New York. Horter added nonetheless, "I am most interested in abstract painting and once owned some very important Picassos but I was not able to keep them — as I had lost a lot of my things during the past 6 years."[69] Among the pictures he had already sold was, apparently, Picasso's *Portrait of Daniel-Henry Kahnweiler*, now in the Art Institute of Chicago.[70] Horter's correspondence with Cooper mentions a total of six pictures: a Gris for which he asked $750; a Braque oval for $600; another Braque oval, *Still Life with Glass and Newspaper* (fig. 20), for which Horter asked $800 and which Cooper bought for £160; a Picasso, *Nude* (fig. 21), for which he asked $800 and Cooper bought for £160; a Picasso negroid figure for $1,500; and a Picasso *papier collé, Still Life with Bottle, Cup and Newspaper* (fig. 22) for which Horter asked $150 and for which Cooper paid £30. In March, April, and May of 1937, therefore, Cooper purchased a total of three works from Horter: a major Braque oil, a major Picasso oil, and a Picasso *papier collé*.[71]

Gottlieb Friedrich Reber

The private collector who undoubtedly exerted the most dramatic impact on Cooper's emerging collection was Gottlieb Friedrich Reber (fig. 23).[72] Reber (1880-1959) was widely acclaimed as a collector, both

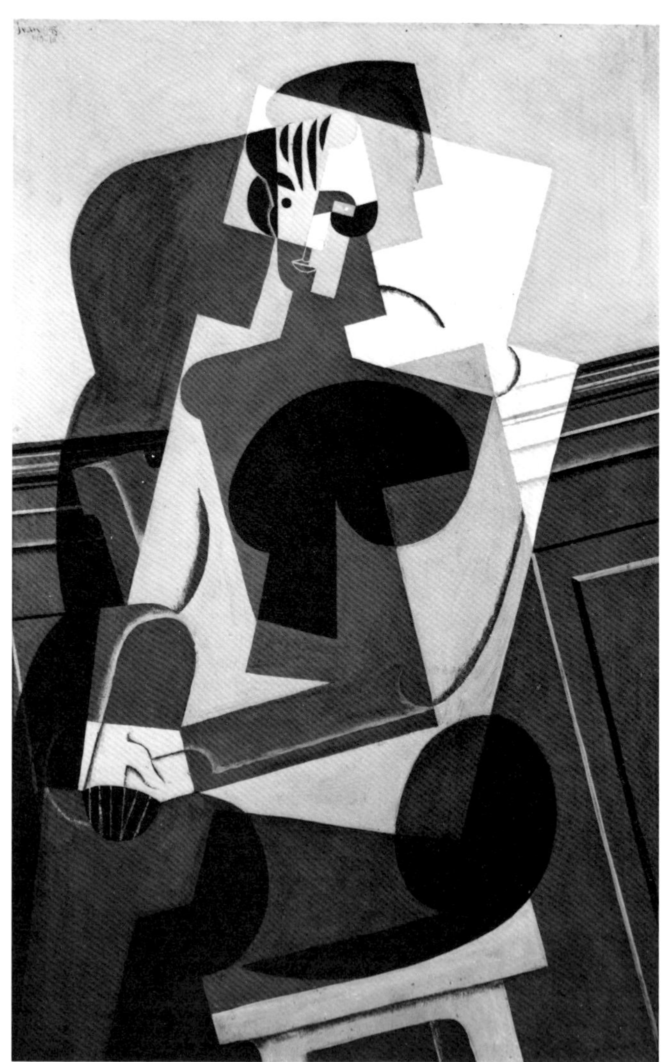

19. Juan Gris, *Portrait of Josette Gris*, 1916, oil on panel, 45½ × 28¾ in. (116 × 73 cm.), Museo del Prado, Madrid.

for his holdings of pictures by nineteenth-century masters, including at least thirty works by Cézanne, and for what was really a second collection of twentieth-century art that focused on Cubism. This included about eighty works by Gris, plus at least seventy oils and innumerable works on paper by Picasso. Cooper purchased fifteen works from Reber in the 1930s and three more between 1944 and 1945.[73]

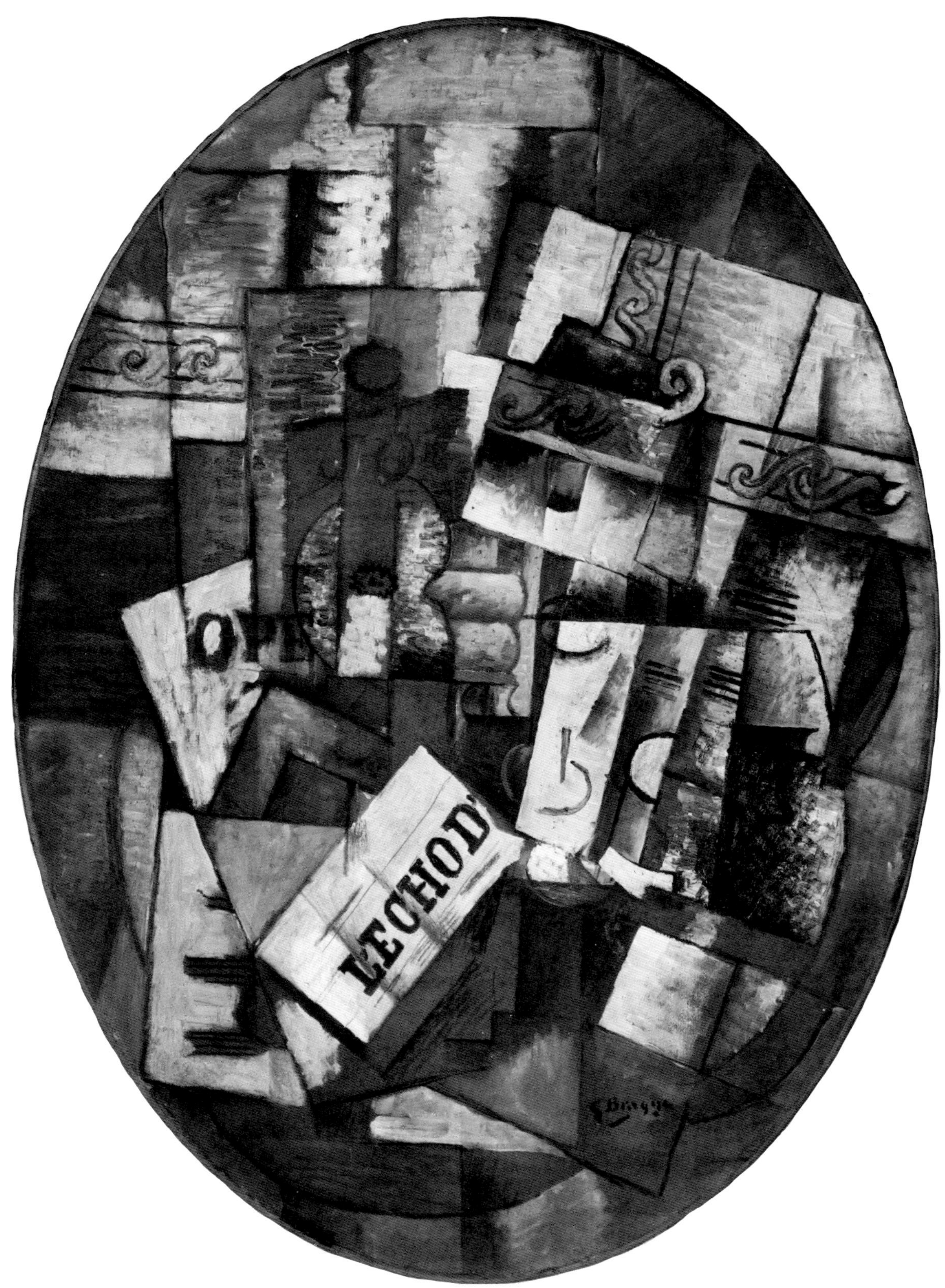

20. Georges Braque, *Still Life with Glass and Newspaper,* Sorgues, summer 1913
oil and charcoal on oval canvas, 38¾ × 28 in. (98.4 × 71.1 cm.), collection Heinz Berggruen, Switzerland.

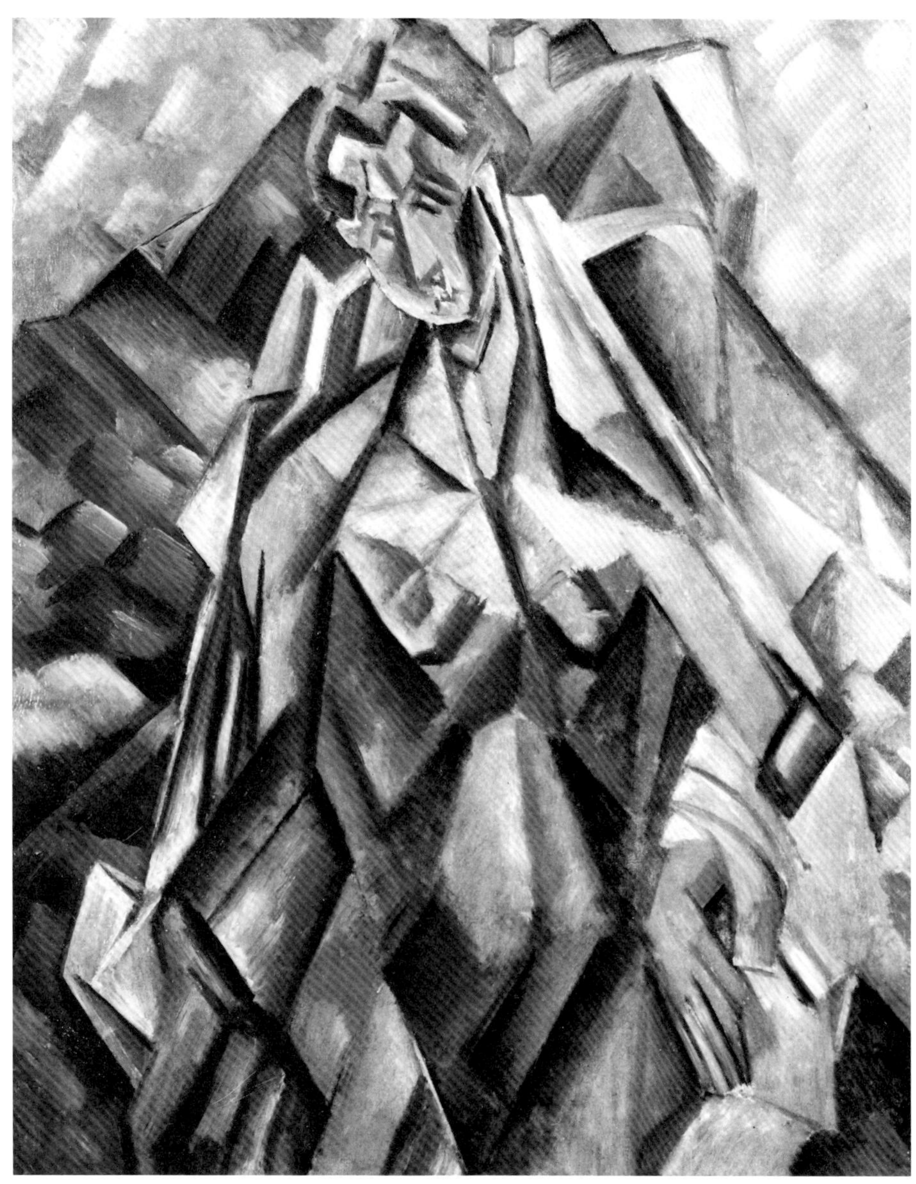

21. Pablo Picasso, *Nude,* 1909, oil on canvas, 35¼ × 28 in. (89.5 × 71.1 cm.), Morton G. Neumann Family Collection.

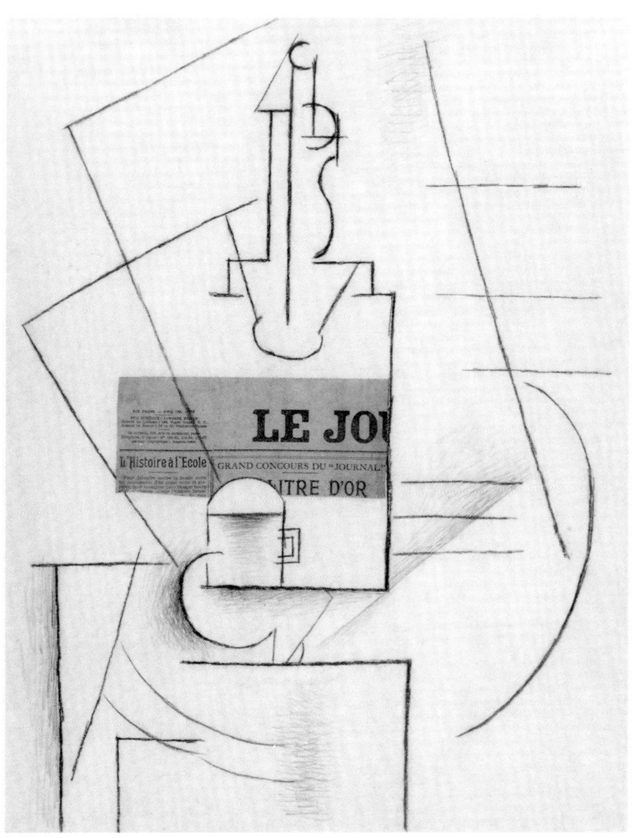

22. Pablo Picasso, *Still Life with Bottle, Cup and Newspaper*, 1912–13, *papier collé*, charcoal, and oil on paper, 24 × 18½ in. (63 × 48 cm.), Museum Folkwang, Essen.

Cooper's purchases of works by Picasso (five oils and eight works on paper) reflect the strength of Reber's Picasso holdings, hailed by Alfred Flechtheim in 1927 as the "decisive Picasso collection."[74] In addition, Cooper purchased from Reber an oil by Braque, *Still Life with a Guitar* (fig. 24), and a major oil by Gris, *Still Life with Guitar on a Table* (fig. 25).[75]

The Picassos purchased from Reber date from 1906 through the 1920s and represent a broad range of the vital stages of the artist's development. *Standing Female Nude* (1906-07), with its aggressive slashing lines of black ink and blotches of red and sepia gouache, relates to the *Demoiselles d'Avignon* in its imposing physicality that appears to challenge the very limits of the sheet.[76] This work reveals the impact of Iberian sculpture and also suggests the influence of Cézanne, particularly his bather compositions.[77] In *Three Figures under a Tree* (winter 1907/08, £900, fig. 26), Picasso combined his fascination with primitive art with dramatic elisions of space, early indications of a crucial Cubist device.[78] The radical geometrization and the colors and patterns of the faceted planes that link landscape, drapery, and figure in *Nude Woman in an Armchair* (fig. 27) are typical of the pictures Picasso executed in Horta during the summer of 1909.[79] Purchased in November 1937, it apparently supplanted the *Nude* purchased from Horter the previous April, a weaker picture that Cooper would sell in 1939. Picasso's 1911/12 *The Clarinet Player* (fig. 28) represents High Analytical Cubism, while the complex pastel *Bottle of "Bass" and Guitar* (1912-13) can be discussed in terms of Synthetic Cubism.[80] Both works are from the period that Cooper himself referred to as "the heroic years of Cubism."[81] Reber seems to have especially favored the monumental nudes of Picasso's neoclassical style of the twenties, and Cooper added two of these to his collection in 1938: the pastel *Two Women* (1920, £500, fig. 29) and the oil *Head of a Woman* (1921, £100).[82] Reber owned the Philadelphia Museum's *Three Musicians* (1921), a culminating work of Picasso's Synthetic Cubist phase. A small related watercolor and pencil drawing, *Woman and Harlequin* (1915), which Cooper purchased in 1938 for £30, reveals a great deal about the development of that Synthetic Cubist vocabulary.[83] Cooper purchased several still lifes from the late 1910s and 1920s, including the large-scale *Still Life on a Table* of 1923-24, purchased for £1,300 (fig. 30).[84]

Reber's impact on Cooper, however, cannot be summed up in a mere list of Cooper's purchases. Rather, it extends more generally to the influence of Reber's circle of friends that Cooper undoubtedly came to know. Reber also contributed to Cooper's basic understanding of collecting and of Cubism. Reber was, in fact, well acquainted with most of the prominent art dealers of the period, including Daniel-Henry Kahnweiler, Paul Cassirer, Léonce and Paul

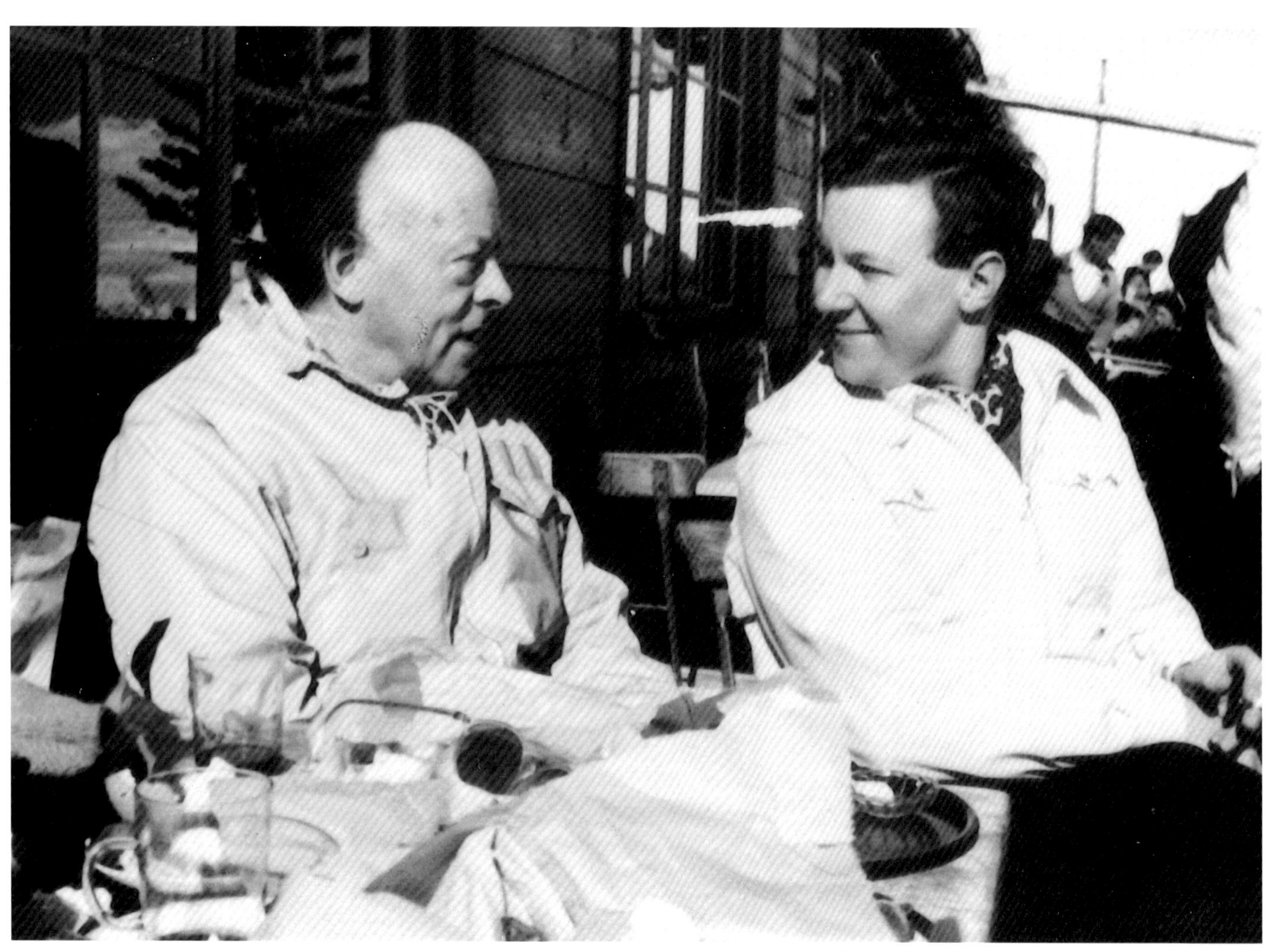

23. G.F. Reber and Douglas Cooper, Arosa, 1938
(Photo, courtesy Elisabeth Eichmann.)

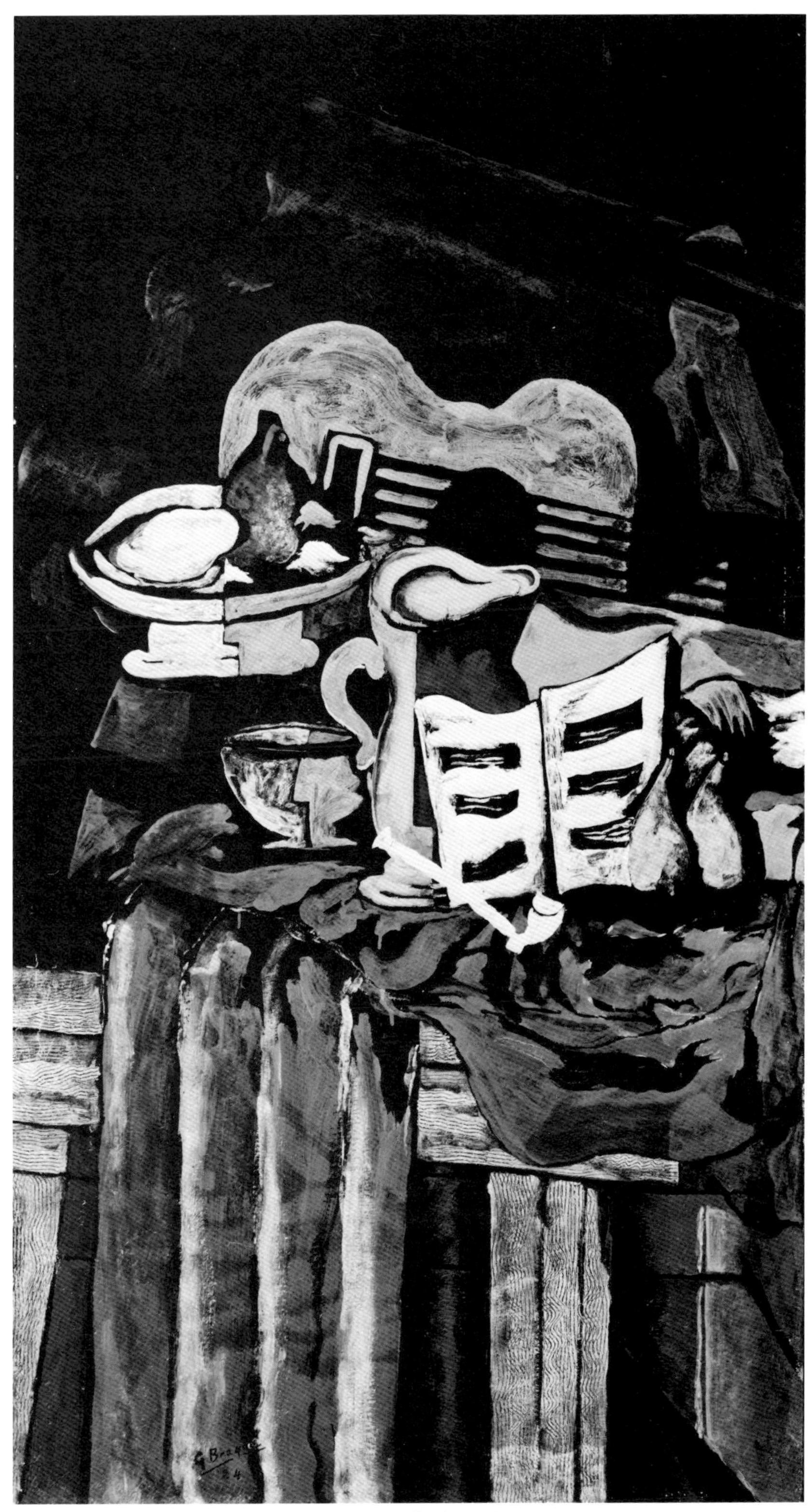

24. Georges Braque, *Still Life with a Guitar,* 1924
oil on canvas, 46½ × 24 in. (118.1 × 61 cm.)
the Jacques and Natasha Gelman Collection, New York.

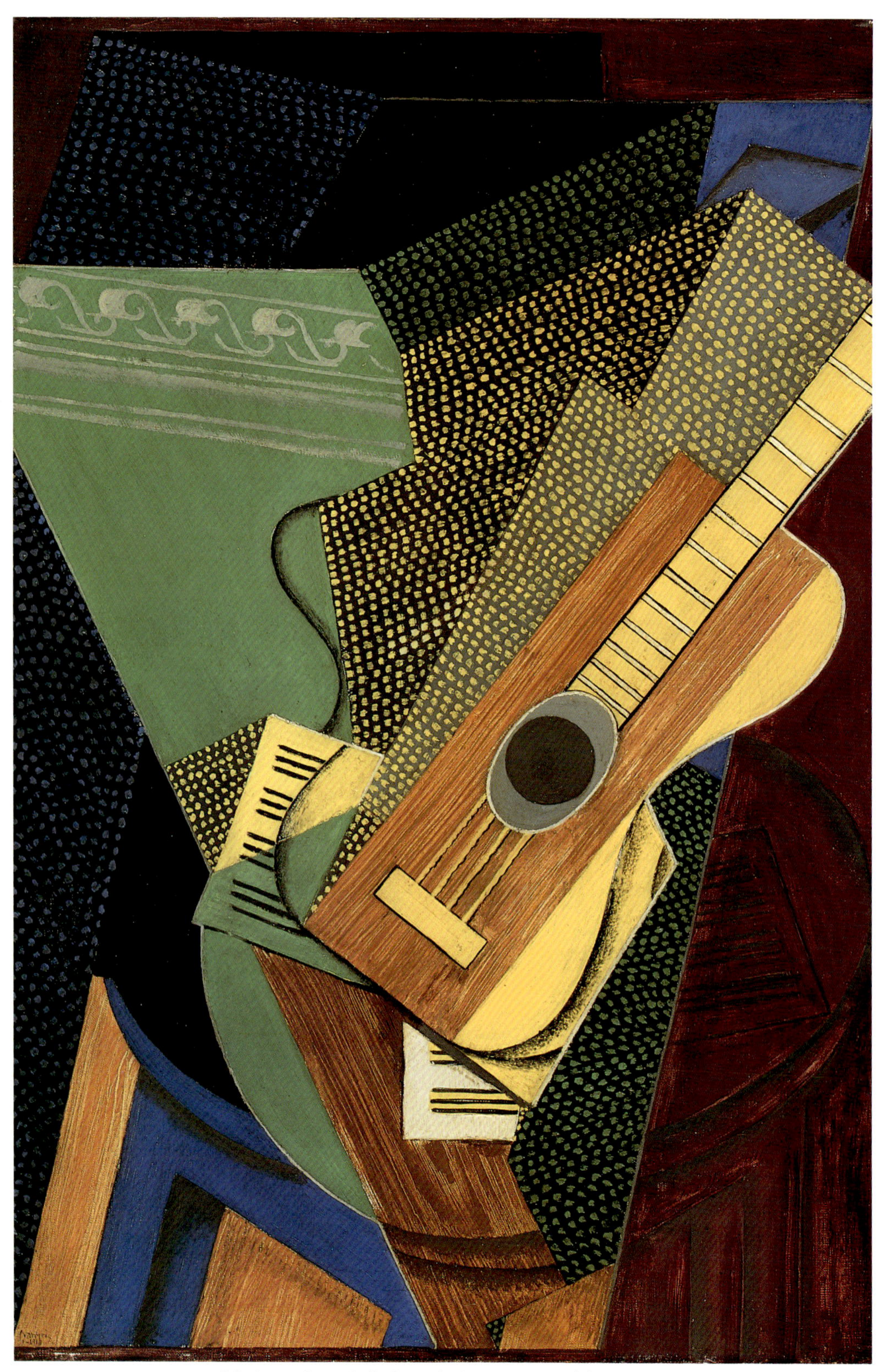

25. Juan Gris, *Still Life with Guitar on a Table,* 1916
oil on canvas, 36 3/16 × 23 3/8 in. (92 × 59.3 cm.), private collection.

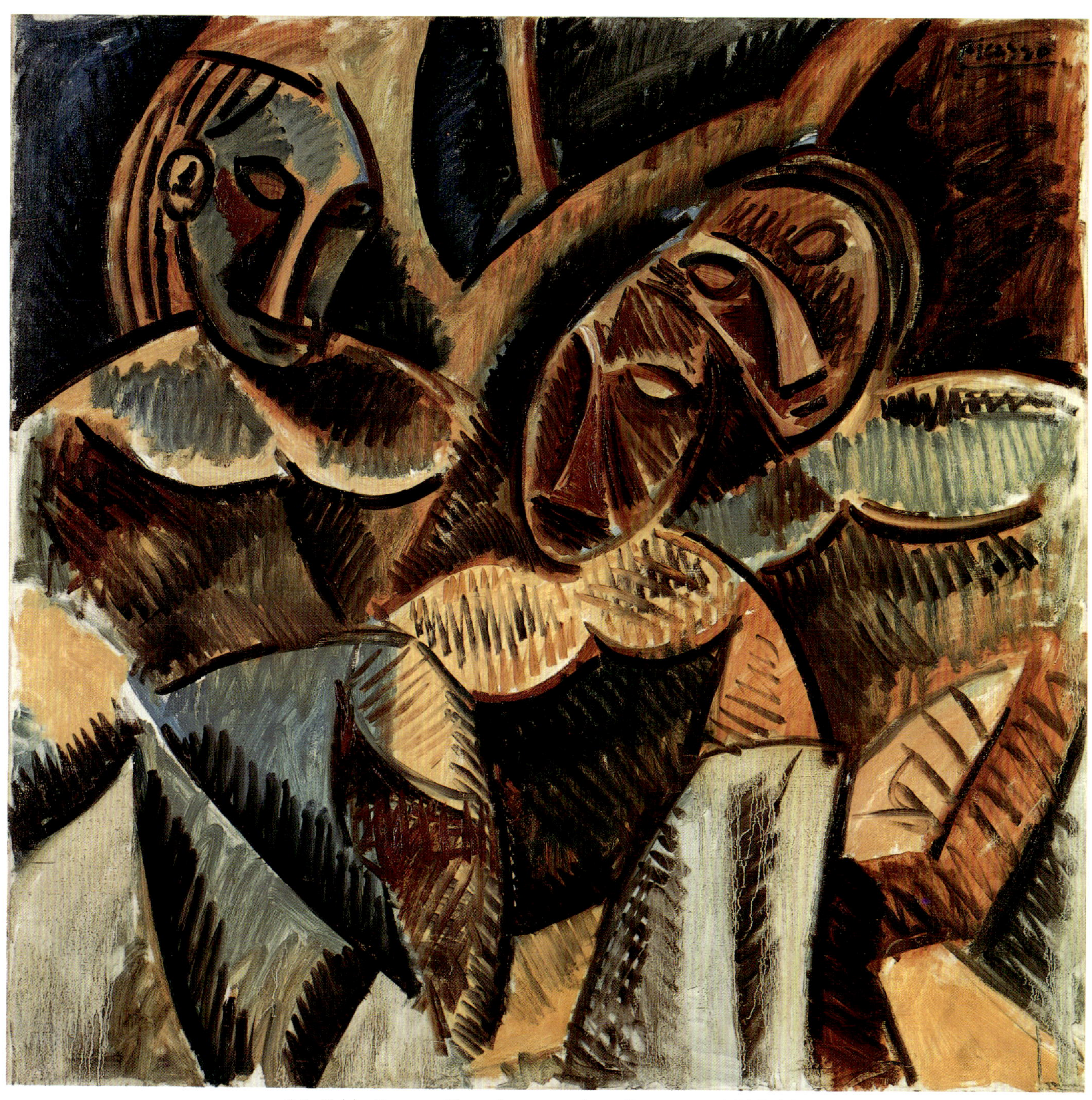

26. Pablo Picasso, *Three Figures under a Tree,* winter 1907–08
oil on canvas, 39 × 39 in. (99 × 99 cm.), Musée Picasso, Paris.

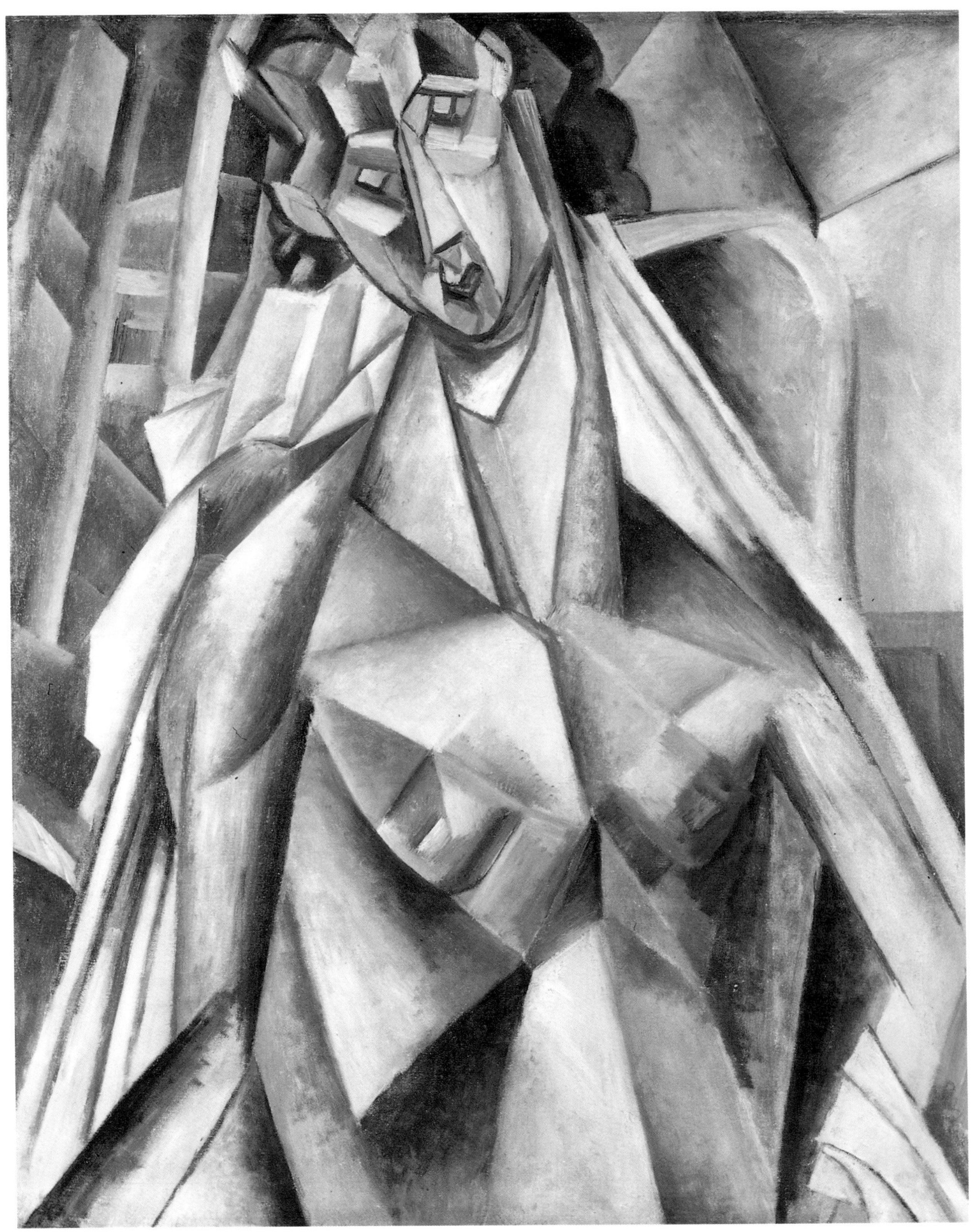

27. Pablo Picasso, *Nude Woman in an Armchair*, summer 1909
oil on canvas, 36½ × 29½ in. (93.5 × 75 cm.), private collection.

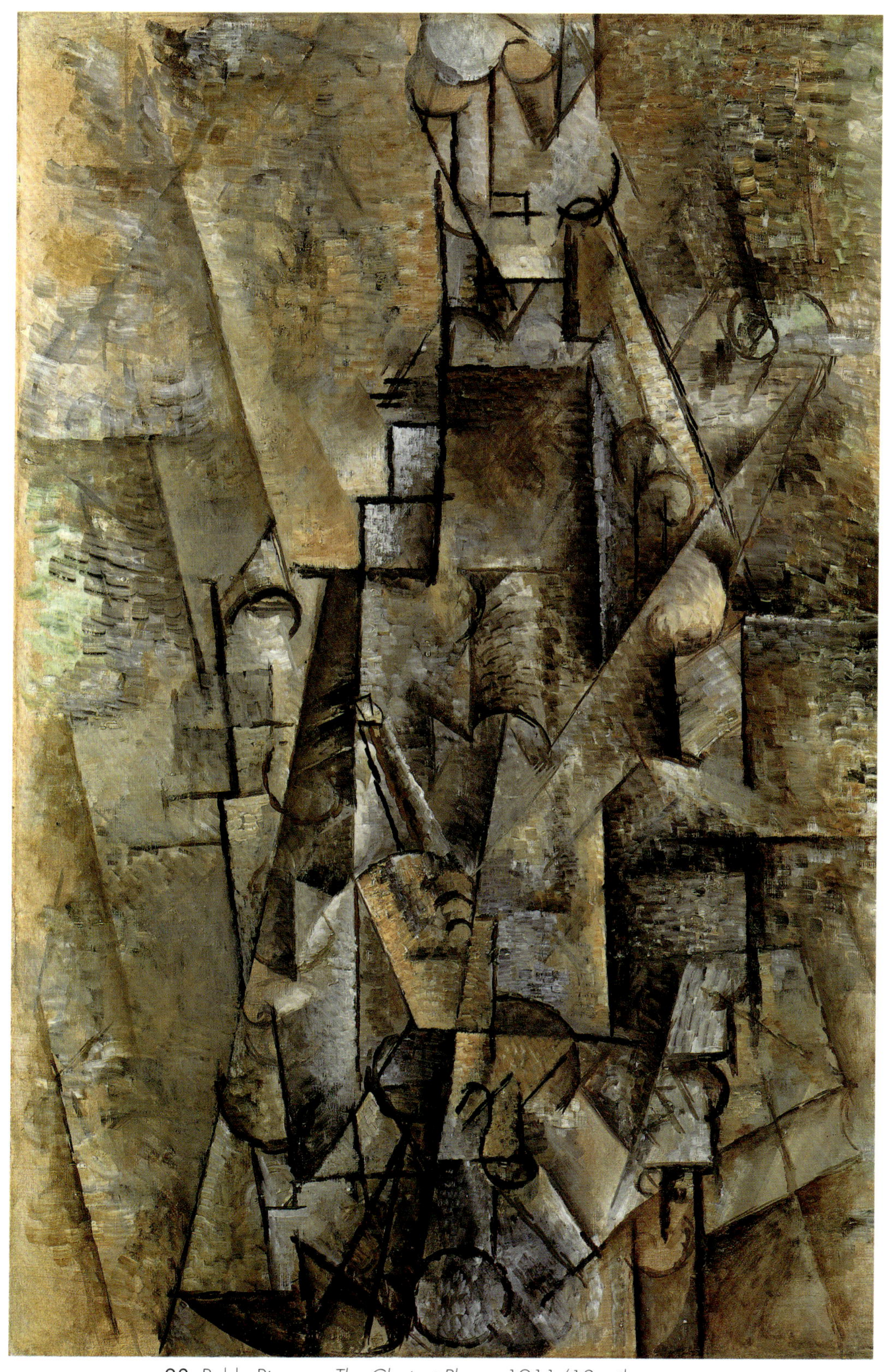

28. Pablo Picasso, *The Clarinet Player,* 1911/12, oil on canvas
43 x 27¼ in. (109 x 69 cm.), Thyssen-Bornemisza Collection, Lugano, Switzerland.

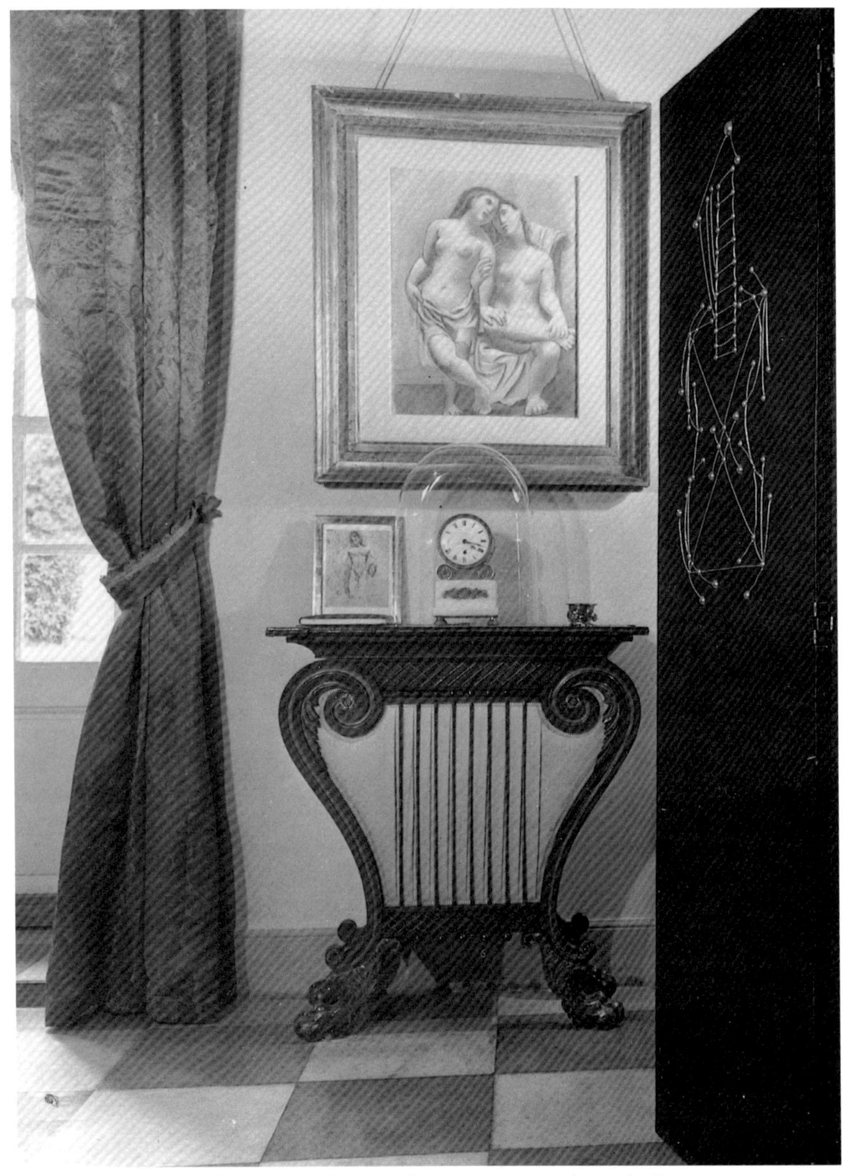

29. Interior of Château de Castille, c. 1955, with works by Picasso: *Two Women*, 1920, pastel on paper; and *Bacchus*, 1908, ink on paper. (Photo, Robert Doisneau.)

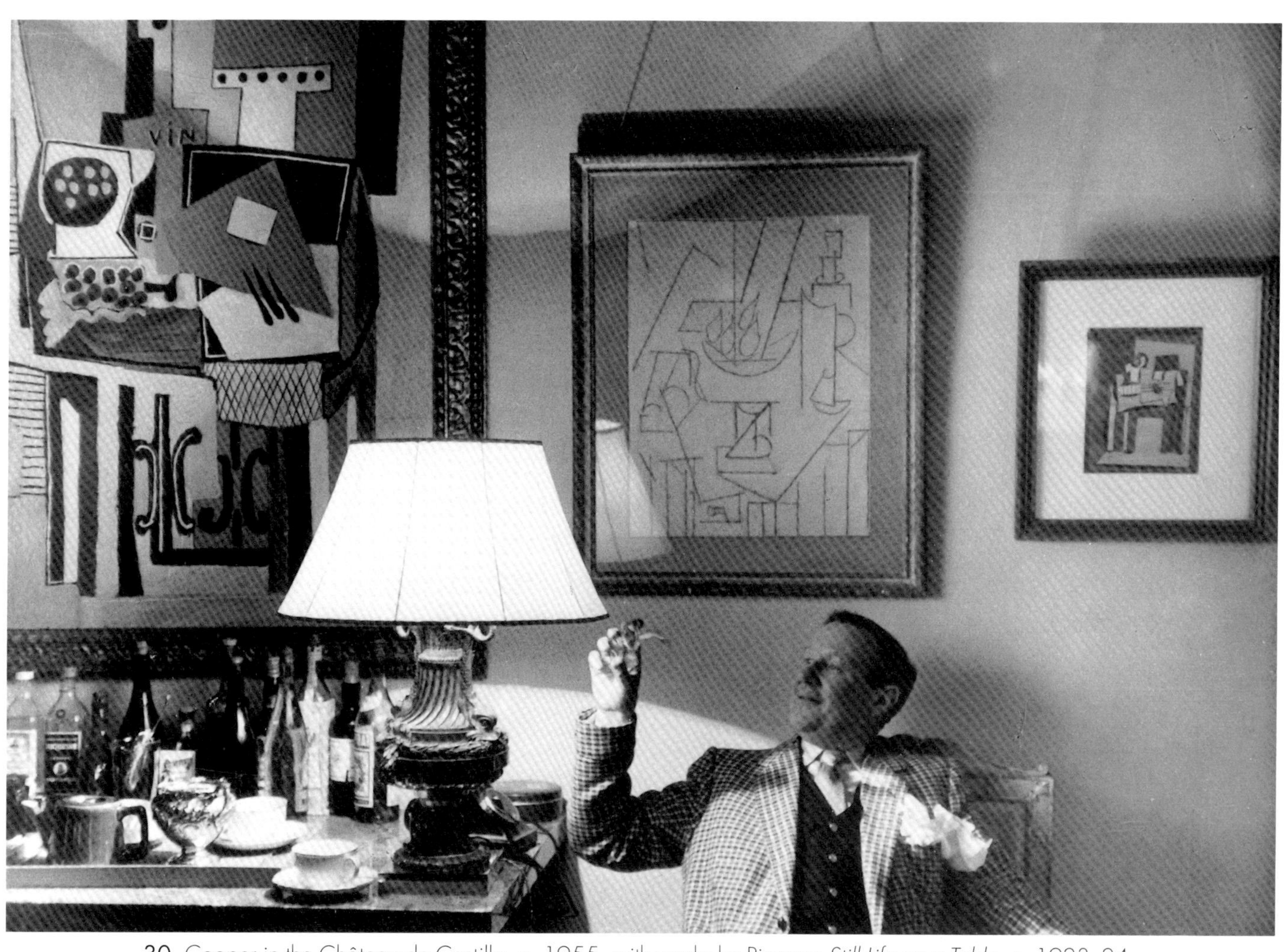

30. Cooper in the Château de Castille, c. 1955, with works by Picasso: *Still Life on a Table,* c. 1923–24, oil on canvas; *Still Life with Table and Dish of Pears,* 1912, pencil and charcoal on paper; and *Still Life with Guitar and Fruit Dish on Table,* 1920, pastel on paper. (Photo, Robert Doisneau.)

Rosenberg, Siegfried Rosengart, and Curt Valentin. Alfred Flechtheim had been a friend of Reber since before World War I, and Reber's *en masse* purchases of works by Juan Gris at the Galerie Simon during the twenties were almost legendary.[85] Reber's collections had been widely exhibited and publicized: in 1913 a selection was shown in Berlin at the Paul Cassirer Gallery and then at the Mathildenhöhe, Darmstadt. Other works were in an exhibition of contemporary art at the Hamburger Kunstverein in 1927.[86] Reber made significant loans to such important presentations as Reid and Lefèvre's *Thirty Years of Picasso* (1931) and the great 1932 Picasso retrospective at Galerie Georges Petit, Paris and the Kunsthaus, Zurich.[87] At the time of his trip to the United States in 1930, even the popular press hailed Reber as the great collector of modern art.[88]

Reber's collection had been praised lavishly not only by Flechtheim, but also by the doyen of nineteenth-century art history, Julius Meier-Graefe, who at the time of his death in 1935 lived in Vevey, not far from Reber's Château de Béthusy in Lausanne.[89] Reber's friend and advisor, the art historian and writer Carl Einstein, effected Reber's conversion to Cubism and his massive purchases of Cubist works. Cooper's own acquaintance with Einstein can be dated to the period between 1928, when Einstein emigrated to Paris, and 1936, when he joined the Republican cause in the Spanish Civil War.[90]

Though relatively unacknowledged today, Einstein was an early and astute champion of Cubism. His noted *Kunst des 20. Jahrhunderts*, first published in 1926 (then reissued in 1928 and 1931) as the sixteenth volume of the noted Propyläen Kunstgeschichte series, included an important and detailed account of Cubism. For a young collector such as Cooper, this volume was a crucial visual resource for Cubist works of art. Einstein apparently helped to secure Reber's prestige as a collector. He dedicated his section on Cubism to Reber, "in herzlicher Freundschaft," and he illustrated seventeen Picassos and seven Braques from Reber's collection.

It seems that as Reber's fortunes waned, Cooper increasingly assumed the role of a preeminent Cubist collector, consciously emulating the older man. There are, in fact, a number of parallels between the two collectors that seem too striking to dismiss as mere coincidence. Cooper's purchase of the Château de Castille in the South of France in the early fifties is reminiscent of Reber's own Château de Béthusy in Lausanne in the 1920s. The frequent visits of artists, dealers, art historians, and critics to Reber in Lausanne is certainly matched three decades later by the evolution of Cooper's Château de Castille into a kind of salon, a veritable pilgrimage stop for members of the art community. Cooper's commission of Léger's *The Trapeze Artists* in 1954 for the stairway landing at Castille also parallels Reber's commission some twenty years earlier of three large-scale works by Léger to decorate his dining room at the Château in Lausanne.

PARIS GALLERIES

Cooper was especially active in Paris, then the center of the avant-garde. There he purchased from and traded with a number of smaller galleries, most of which had sprouted up during the boom years of the 1920s and were located in Montparnasse.[91] He bought extensively from Galerie Pierre, Galerie Jeanne Bucher, Galerie Percier, Galerie Zak, Galerie de Beaune, and Galerie Renou & Colle. Along with the more established dealer Kahnweiler and his Galerie Simon, or Léonce Rosenberg and his Galerie de l'Effort Moderne, these newer establishments constituted a major source of Cubist art for Cooper.

Galerie Pierre

Galerie Pierre was located first on 13, rue Bonaparte; later at 14, rue de Seine; and as of 1936, at 1, rue des Beaux-Arts. It was owned by Pierre Loeb (1897-1964), who championed especially the Surrealists.[92] He showed works by Alberto Giacometti, Masson, Miró, Hans Arp, Ernst, Wolfgang Paalen, and Victor Brauner. One of the most notable exhibitions was *La Peinture surréaliste*, for which André Breton and Robert Desnos wrote prefaces to the catalogue. Held in

November, 1925, the exhibition included works by Giorgio de Chirico, Ernst, Klee, Man Ray, Masson, Picasso, and Pierre Roy.

After his anomalous purchase of the Cézanne from Loeb in 1933, Cooper acquired eleven works by Miró, Picasso, Braque, and Léger from the dealer between 1936 and 1938. These included three 1935 gouaches by Miró that Cooper purchased in 1936 for £6, £14, and £14.[93] In 1937 he bought a recent Miró ink drawing for £8.[94] In June 1937 he purchased three gouaches on paper by Léger dating from 1913 and 1914 for £5 each, including *Still Life on a Table* (1914, fig. 31); these reveal Cooper's concentrated pursuit of Léger's pre-World War I *contrastes de formes*.[95] At the same time, Cooper purchased a 1913 *papier collé* by Georges Braque (£25).[96] In November 1936 he bought a Picasso 1912-13 pencil drawing for £25, and in February 1938, *Head of a Man*, a 1908 ink and charcoal drawing by Picasso, for £20.[97] Cooper's final purchase from Loeb, in May 1938 for £150, was Picasso's 1918 oil *Still Life with Garlands* (fig. 2).[98] With the exception of Cooper's Cézanne oil, this was the most expensive purchase from Loeb.

Cooper's long-standing fascination with Miró may well have been inspired by Loeb, who already in 1925 had championed the artist. Loeb presented Miró's work in a one-person exhibition that became a *succès de scandale*, and especially attracted the interest of the Surrealists.[99]

The primary source, however, for Cooper's collection of works by Miró (altogether about twenty-one works, including four oils) was the Pierre Matisse Gallery in New York. Matisse had represented Miró in New York since the artist's first exhibition there, held November 1 to 25, 1932. In 1936 and 1937 Cooper purchased eleven works by Miró, with prices ranging from £14 to £150; these include his *Catalan Peasant Resting* of 1936.[100] Cooper's enthusiasm for Miró was not short-lived: twelve of the nineteen major works by Miró purchased in the thirties remained in Cooper's collection well into the 1960s, and he devoted a room at the Château de Castille to Miró's work.[101] Cooper also bought from Pierre Matisse a work by Gris for £200, and *The Student* (1917-18), an important Picasso, for £600 (fig. 32).[102]

Galerie Jeanne Bucher

Pierre Loeb's association with Jeanne Bucher (1872-1945) and her nearby gallery is consistent with the close relationships among this group of contemporary art dealers.[103] Like Loeb, Bucher exhibited the Surrealists and the Cubists, and she vigorously championed younger artists such as Charles Lapicque. The French painter and designer Jean Lurçat (1892-1966), whom she met during her stay in Switzerland after World War I, was apparently an important influence on Bucher. He introduced her to a lively circle of artists and writers including Arp, Ernst, and Jacques Lipchitz, and to the various collectors who supported her efforts with her new gallery in Paris.[104]

In May 1937 Cooper bought a 1919 Gris drawing from the Galerie Bucher for £15, and in February 1938 he bought two more Gris drawings from Bucher, paying £10 for each. These three pencil drawings by Gris included his *Still Life: Teapot and Glass* (1916) and *Still Life: The Tobacco Pouch* (1918).[105] They expanded Cooper's collection of five works by Gris purchased in 1935 from the Zoubaloff sale, the purchases from Flechtheim in 1935, those from Zak in January 1936, from Kahnweiler in November 1936, and from Pierre Matisse in March 1937, and the two works from the Pertuisot sale at Christie's in April of 1937. Cooper's Gris collection continued to expand rapidly in 1937, including purchases in June and November from Kahnweiler (£100 and £170).

Cooper continued assiduously to build his collection of Légers. At the Rains Galleries, 12-14 E. 49th St. in New York, on February 5, 1937, he purchased at auction the pencil study for *Curtain for La Création du monde* (£10, fig. 33).[106] In 1937 he also bought drawings by Léger (£5 each), including *Man and Dog in a Landscape* (fig. 34), which may have been part of the Léger exhibition that Bucher held from April 30 to May 14 of that year. *The Mason* was another of the drawings bought that year. *Les Foreurs* (£5) was the first of Léger's war drawings that Cooper added to his collection. In December 1937 he purchased two additional drawings from Léonce Rosenberg for £4, both relating to Léger's major canvas *The Cardplayers* (1917), now

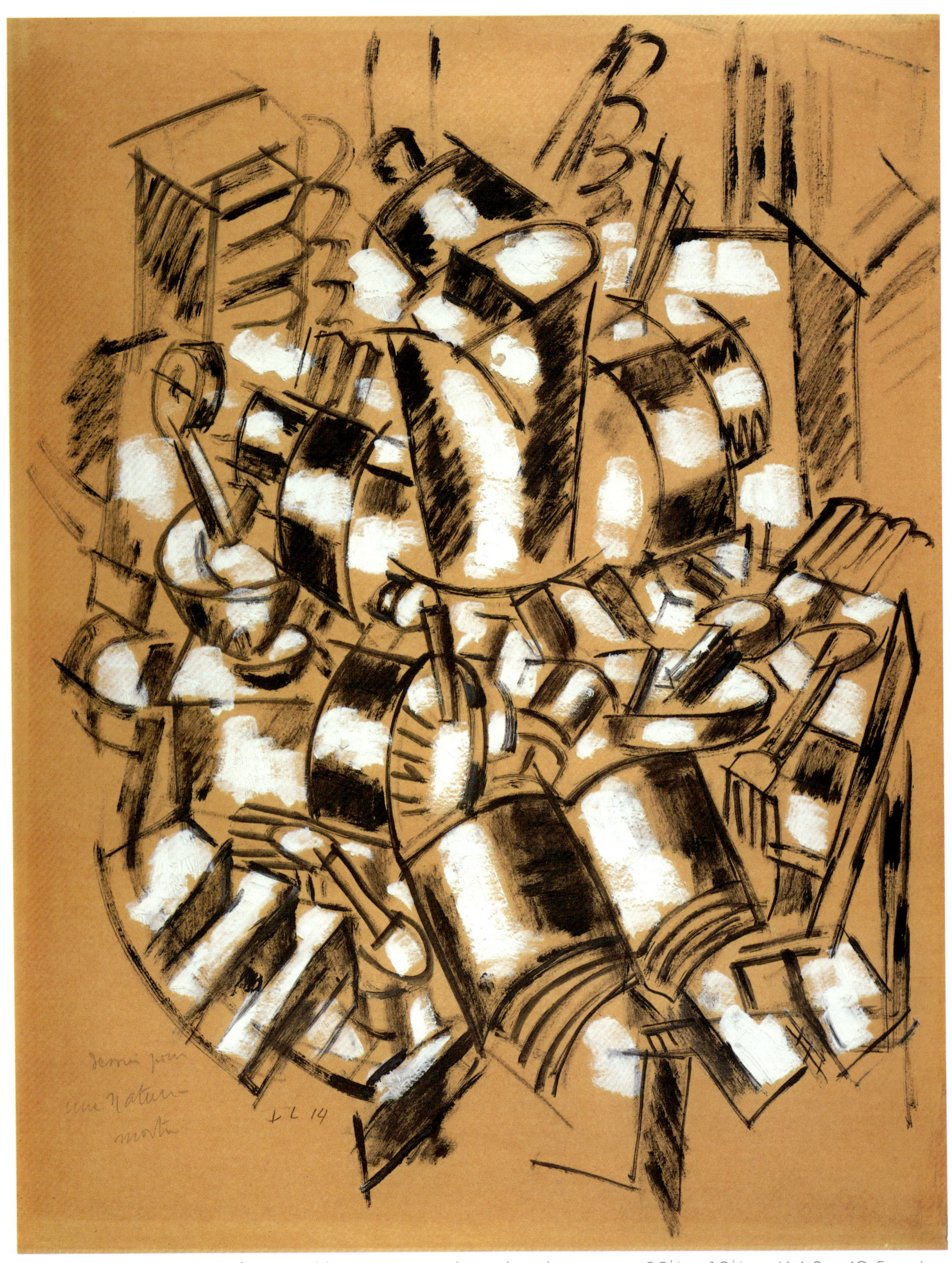

31. Fernand Léger, *Still Life on a Table,* 1914, gouache and wash on paper, $25\frac{1}{2} \times 19\frac{1}{2}$ in. (64.8 × 49.5 cm.) The Metropolitan Museum of Art, New York; gift of Mr. and Mrs. William R. Acquavella, 1986.396.2.

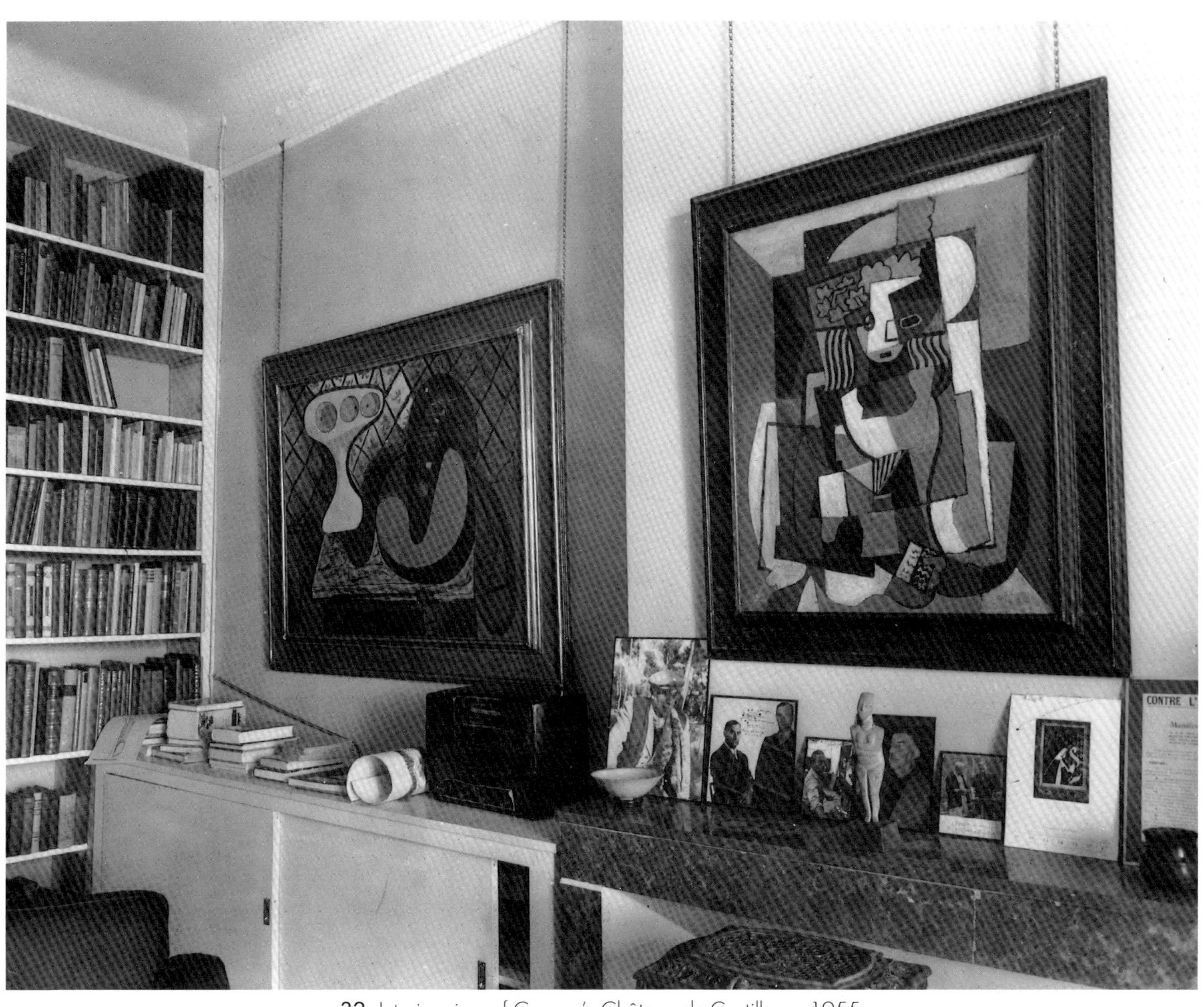

32. Interior view of Cooper's Château de Castille, c. 1955,
with Pablo Picasso's *Still Life with Fruit Dish and Mandolin,* 1932, oil on canvas;
and *The Student,* 1917–18, oil on canvas.

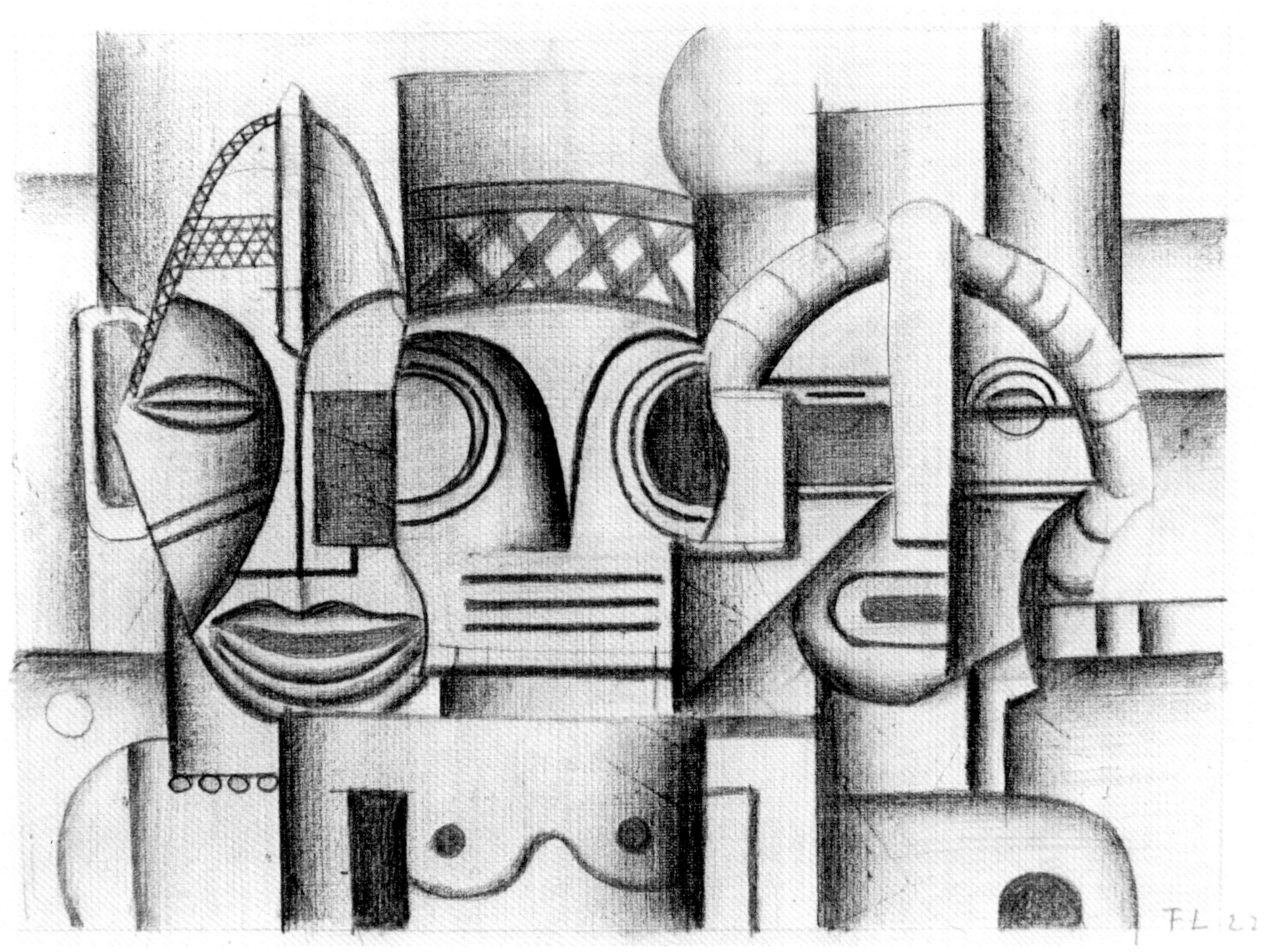

33. Fernand Léger, Study for *Curtain for La Création du monde,* 1922
pencil on paper, 7½ × 9⅞ in. (25 × 19 cm.), Jean-Claude Bellier.

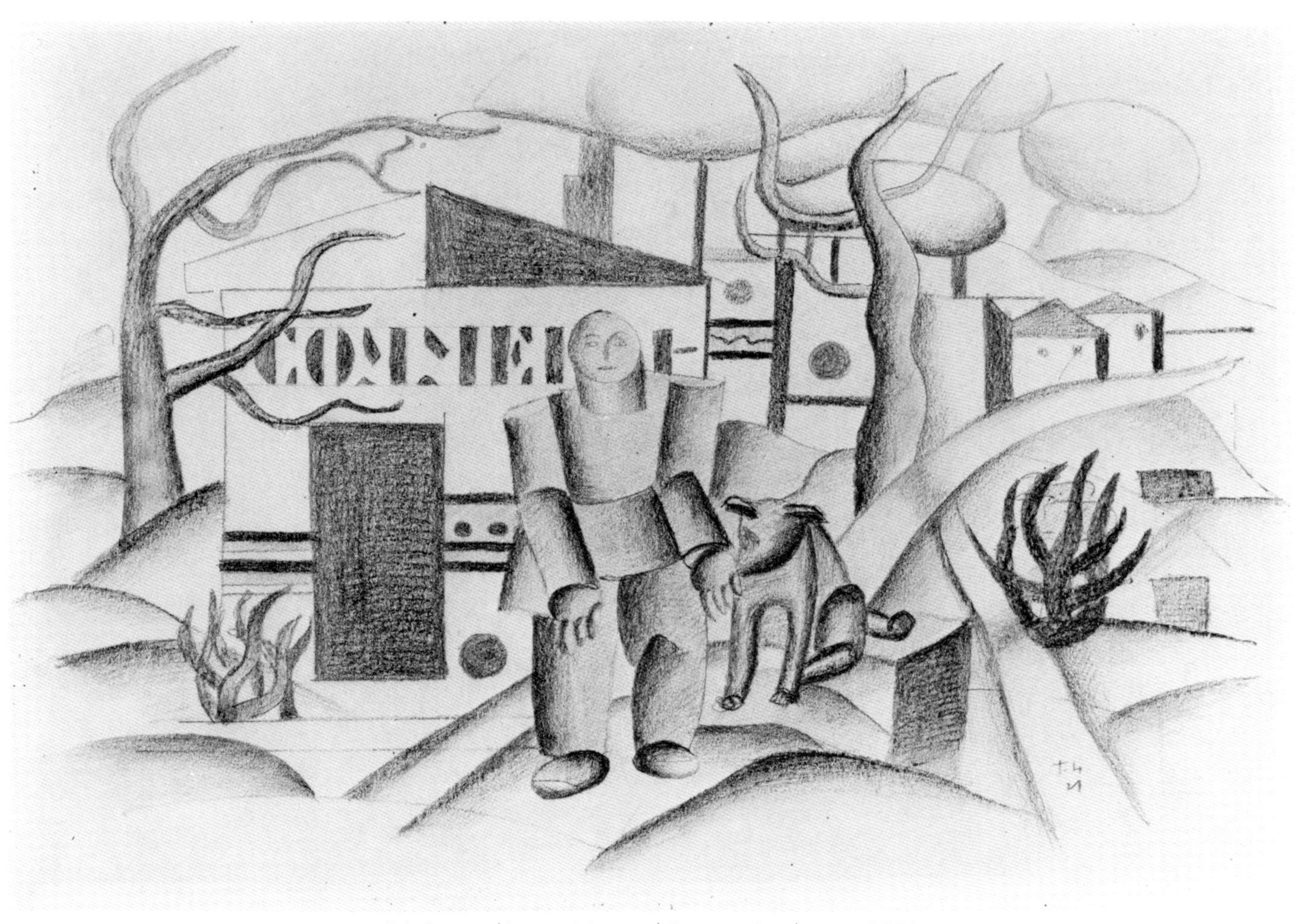

34. Fernand Léger, *Man and Dog in a Landscape,* 1921
pencil on paper, $10\frac{3}{16} \times 14\frac{7}{8}$ in. (26.2 × 37.9 cm.),
The Museum of Ulm, Permanent Loan from the State of Baden-Württemberg.

at the Kröller-Müller Museum in Otterlo.[107] Cooper's interest in this particular phase of Léger's work was manifested years later in subsequent purchases, as well as in his publication in 1956 of *Fernand Léger, dessins de la guerre, 1915-16.*[108]

Galerie Percier

Jeanne Bucher had been associated with the Peau de l'Ours, the well-known group initiated and organized primarily by André Level that functioned as a kind of art syndicate.[109] After the first World War, Level's Galerie Percier on the rue de la Boëtie was conceived somewhat after the Peau de l'Ours, for it depended on the financial support of a small group of private collectors and investors with enthusiasm for contemporary art.[110] Level was an executive of a company controlling the docks in Marseilles, and his associates included André Lefèvre, an important figure in banking and investment, and Alfred Richet, secretary of a coal import company. The economic positions of these men were secure enough that they could champion an art form as controversial as Cubism.[111] Cooper made three purchases from Level, the most important of which was the Juan Gris oil *Houses on the Place Ravignan, Paris* (1911, fig. 35), for which he paid £50 in February 1938.[112]

Galerie Zak

Provenance history reveals that Level had obtained the Gris *Houses on the Place Ravignan, Paris* from the Polish dealer Eugène Zak (1884-1926), a painter in his own right.[113] Zak was also a collector and maintained a gallery at 16, rue de l'Abbaye during the 1930s, where he exhibited works by other Eastern European artists and, occasionally, his own works. In addition, he maintained a regular schedule of exhibitions that featured, among others, Georges Rouault, Amedeo Modigliani, André Derain, Picasso, and Maurice Utrillo. In January 1936 Cooper purchased a 1913 Gris watercolor and charcoal from Zak for £18.[114]

Galerie de Beaune

Galerie de Beaune at 25, rue de Beaune was the source of another important canvas by Gris, *Portrait of the Artist's Mother* (1912, fig. 36). Cooper purchased this picture in June 1938 for £65.[115] The management of the Galerie de Beaune is now possible to identify. According to letterhead from 1938-39, the principals of the gallery were Edwin Livengood and Georges Maratier. Before Maratier directed it, the Galerie de Beaune may have been owned at one time by Léonce Rosenberg. There was also apparently a later connection with the Galerie Percier, because Livengood became the director of that gallery, where he succeeded André Level.[116]

Maratier clearly had a friendly acquaintance or a close friendship with Cooper. A letter from Maratier at the Galerie de Beaune to Cooper, datable by its contents to late 1938 or early 1939, offers a number of interesting details.[117] The letter shows that Maratier seems to have been asked to intercede with Cooper in order to secure the loan of a Gris in Cooper's collection (this surely was the *Portrait of the Artist's Mother* sold to Cooper already in June 1938) for an exhibition at the Bern Kunsthalle held from May 6 to June 14, 1939. Maratier's account of the difficulties surrounding the sale of another picture apparently owned by Reber emphasizes the complexity of Reber's situation, and reveals as well the close interaction of these collectors and dealers. Perhaps most significant in the context of this examination of Cooper's collecting during the 1930s is Maratier's dogged optimism in the face of an art market that had ground to a complete standstill.

Galerie Renou & Colle

Another important gallery of contemporary art was Renou & Colle. Pierre Colle (d. 1949) and Maurice Renou (c. 1898-1973) associated to form this gallery about 1935. Previously Colle had maintained a gallery at 29, rue Cambacérès, exhibiting Degas, Matisse, Derain, Picasso, Braque, André Dunoyer de Segonzac, and R.-N.-F. de La Fresnaye. He held particularly close relationships with the Surrealists, and through the early 1930s he organized important exhibitions of their work.[118] His connections with such aristocratic collectors as the Vicomte and Vicomtesse de Noailles and

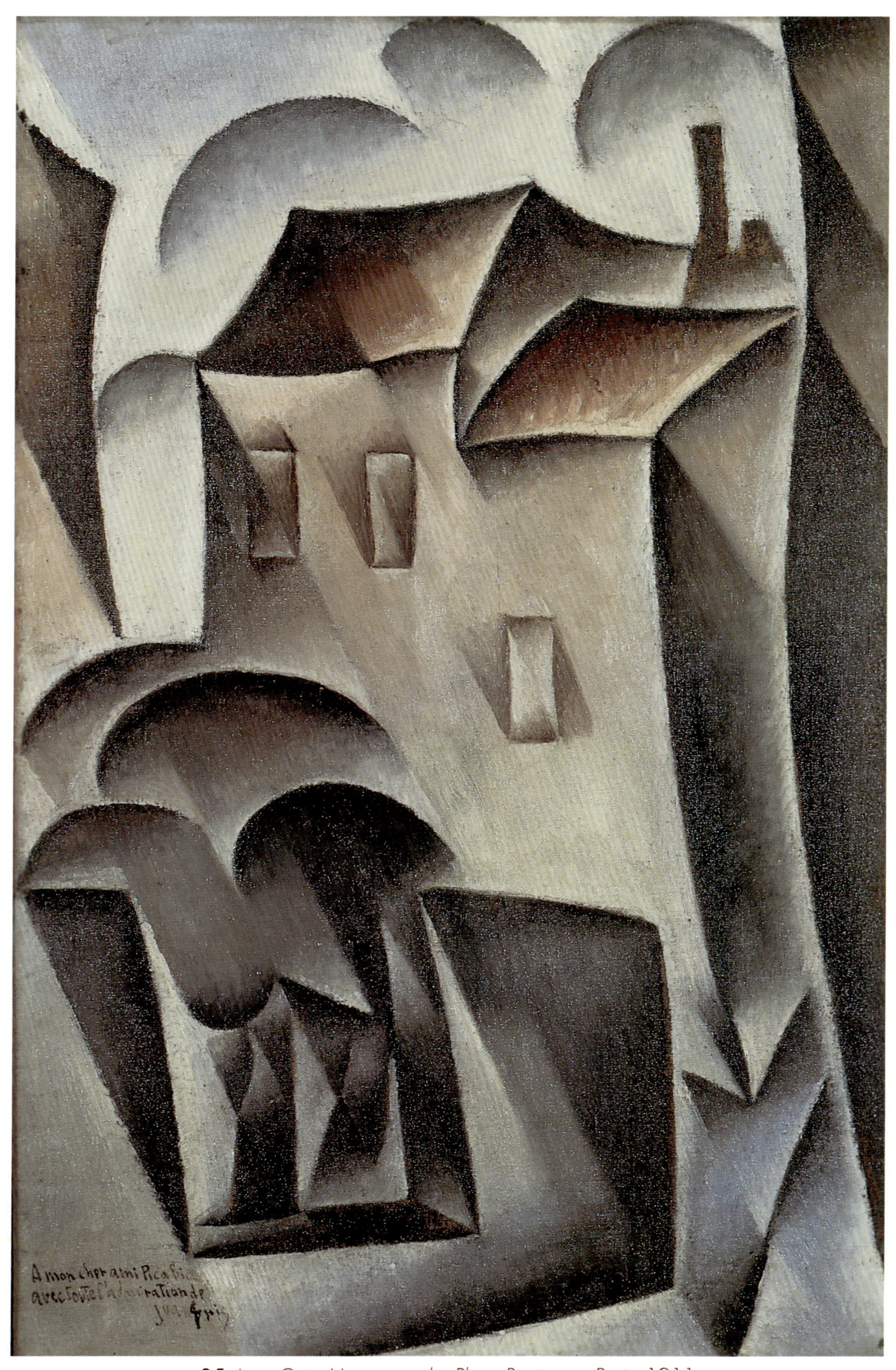

35. Juan Gris, *Houses on the Place Ravignan, Paris,* 1911, oil on canvas, 20½ × 13⅜ in. (52 × 34 cm.), private collection.

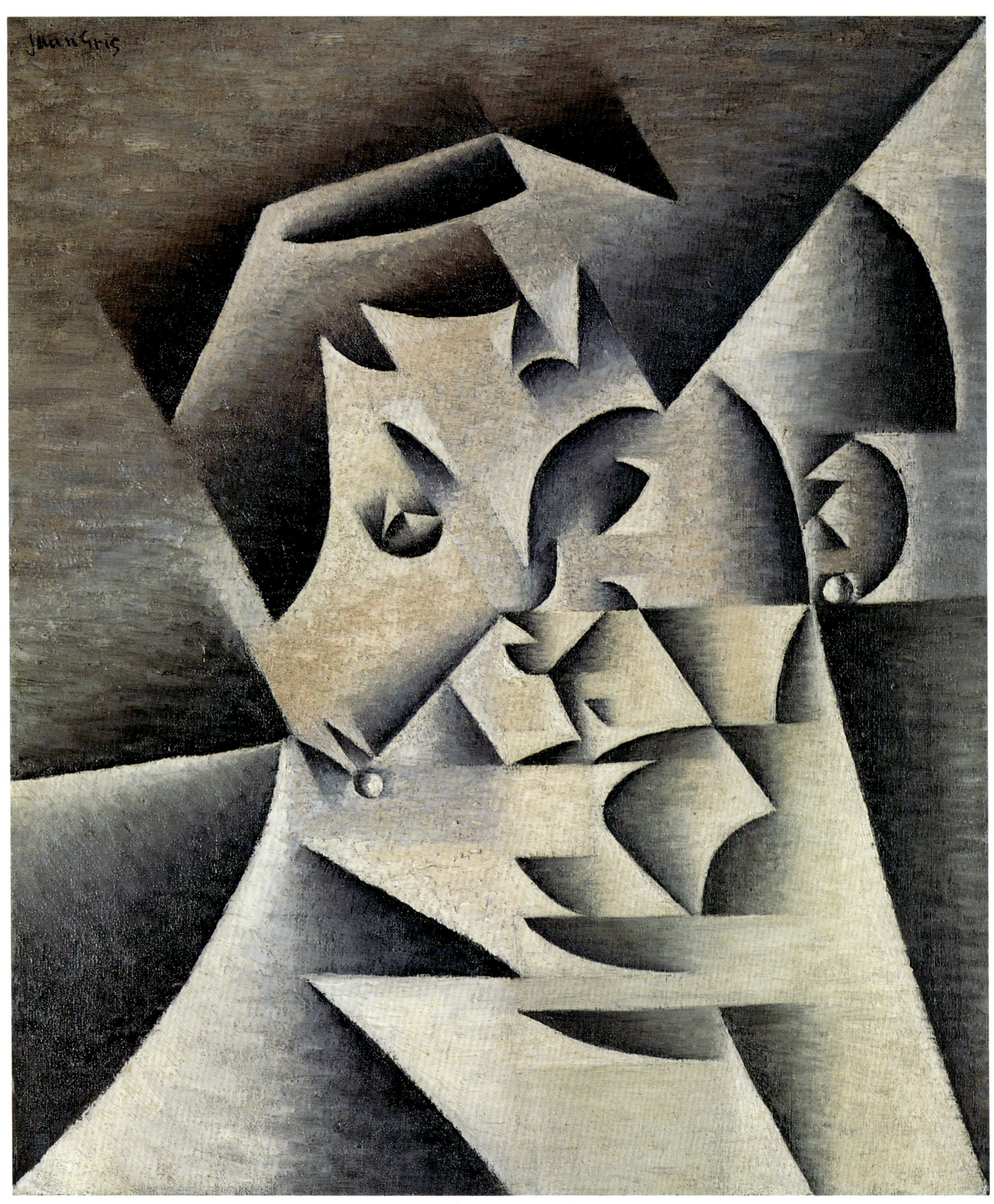

36. Juan Gris, *Portrait of the Artist's Mother*, c. March 1912
oil on canvas, $21\frac{13}{16} \times 18\frac{1}{4}$ in. (55.4 × 46.3 cm.), private collection.

the Comte and Comtesse de Beaumont helped to make the gallery a financial success.

Renou had ties with the Renoir family, for whom he catalogued the contents of the Impressionist's atelier and handled the sale of paintings by other artists as well. By 1935, Renou and Colle had opened their gallery at 164, rue de Faubourg St. Honoré. Theirs was an important gallery dealing extensively in works by Picasso and by the Surrealists.[119] Besides Cooper, their clients included Valentine Dudensing, Albert Skira, Georges Salle, Peter Watson, Raoul La Roche, Paul Rosenberg, Albert Sarrault, Edward James, the Leicester Gallery, and Alfred Barr. Moreover, gallery records indicate that Renou and Colle were active members of what was clearly a very tightly knit community of dealers in especially Parisian, but also international, contemporary art.[120] A number of their purchases were made in conjunction with Pierre Loeb, Edwin Livengood, and George Maratier of the Galerie de Beaune, or from the ubiquitous Dr. Reber.[121]

Douglas Cooper purchased three Picasso drawings from Renou and Colle which may have been included in the February 14 to March 11, 1936 exhibition at the gallery. These were *Standing Woman* (1911-12, £10), *The Card Player* (1914, £12), and *Still Life with Table and Dish of Pears* (1912, £15, fig. 30).[122]

1939—WAR

The outbreak of World War II in September 1939 brought the art trade to an abrupt halt. This is communicated dramatically through the examination of an art journal such as *Beaux-Arts*. This weekly publication, which always included a detailed calendar of art exhibitions in Paris and abroad, had an abrupt hiatus in 1939 after the August 25 issue, with only three more issues appearing that year. Dated November 15, December 1, and December 15, these issues are filled with features of general cultural interest and stories relating to the war, for example an article on the evacuation of the contents of the art museum in Basel. Lively reportage about the art scene was replaced with "Nouvelles de tous," a lengthy section devoted to brief lines noting war-related details such as information concerning the whereabouts or military status of people in the art world. The magazine reappeared twice monthly from January 1 to June 1, 1940, when it shut down permanently.

During the remaining precarious months of the 1930s, Cooper's own collecting screeched to an equally sudden halt. His purchases concluded in the first half of 1939 demonstrate that even before the war there was already a clear shift in the market. He made no purchases in Paris in 1939, except perhaps five pen-and-ink drawings by Léger, relating to his *Composition with Two Parrots*, which Cooper bought directly from the artist (£5 each, fig. 37). The case was different, however, outside of the Continent and in neutral Switzerland. Cooper bought eight works in England and Switzerland in 1939. From Reber in Lausanne he obtained four works by Picasso. One of these (*Bacchus*, fig. 29) was a gift. *Bottle of "Bass" and Guitar* was bought for £100, and two others were purchased for unrecorded prices. A Gris oil, *Still Life with Guitar on a Table* (£300), was also purchased from Reber.[123] The remaining three works were also by Gris: an oil from the collector and dealer Willi Raeber in Basel (£80), and another oil (£20) as well as a *papier collé, Still Life with Bottle and Cigars* (£10), both from the decorator Ronald Fleming in London.[124] By 1939-40, however, the spread of the war forced the entire European art market, including its Parisian center, virtually to shut down.[125]

Cooper remained in France after the outbreak of war, and was ultimately awarded a military medal for his services with a French ambulance unit organized by fellow collector Comte Etienne de Beaumont.[126] On his return to England, Cooper served in the intelligence branch of the Royal Air Force. From 1944 to 1946 he was a consultant for the Monuments and Fine Arts Branch, Control Commission for Germany, helping to repatriate confiscated works of art and to identify important works of art and architecture to be protected from destruction.

Cooper's wartime service certainly left no opportunity for collecting. No purchases are recorded for 1940, 1941, or 1942, and only one is indicated for each of the

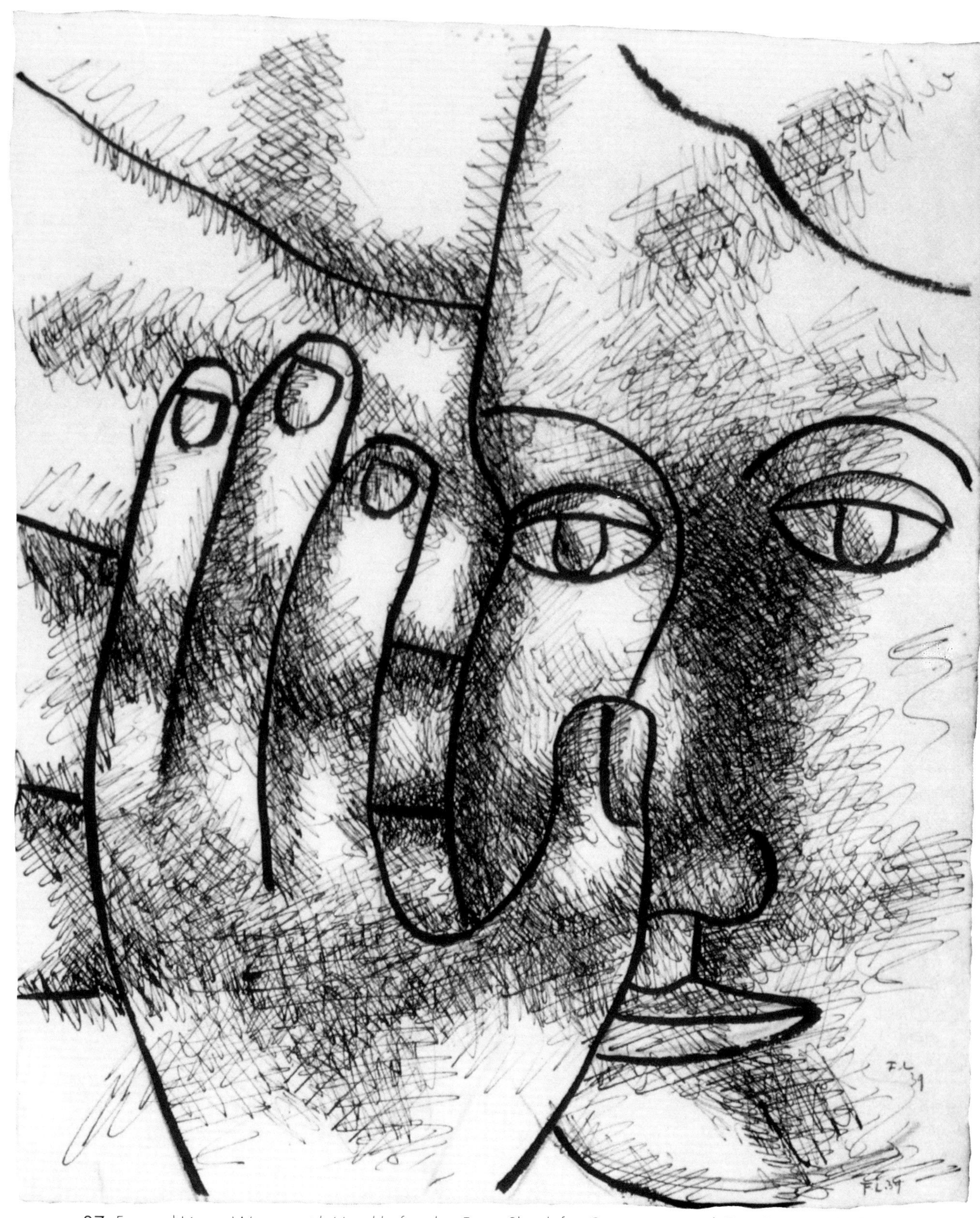

37. Fernand Léger, *Woman with Hand before her Face*, Sketch for *Composition with Two Parrots*, 1939
pen and ink on paper, 15⅜ × 12⅝ in. (39.4 × 32.1 cm.), private collection.

next two years. Both of these works were bought in London: in 1943 he bought Braque's *Still Life: Fruit Dish and Newspaper* for £25 from the Redfern Gallery and in 1944, a Picasso, *Nude*, for £50 from Freddy H. Mayor.[127]

As an indirect result of Cooper's service with the Arts Commission, and especially through his contacts in Switzerland, Cooper acquired perhaps another eight works by Paul Klee, either from the newly formed Klee Gesellschaft or directly from Klee's widow, Lillie. Between 1945 and 1949 Cooper purchased or was given at least fifteen works by Klee. This interest in Klee, as we have seen, can be traced to Flechtheim's influence and to the one-person exhibitions organized in 1934 and 1935 at the Mayor Gallery.[128]

When Cooper's collecting began to resume in 1945, his activities remained focused in London, Lausanne, Basel, and Bern. From Reid & Lefèvre in London he acquired a 1912 Léger oil, *View of Paris* (£200, fig. 8).[129] A watercolor and pencil drawing by Modigliani from 1919 was purchased at St. George's Gallery in London for £100.[130]

Cooper's acquisition of works from Reber's collection after 1945 must be seen in the context of Reber's difficult political and financial situation.[131] Reber had been in Italy since 1940 or 1941, where he explored the few remaining possibilities the art market left open, delved into Old Master paintings, and for a brief period in 1941, assisted the Germans with their art collecting. Reber subsequently found himself out of favor with the Germans and stripped of his German citizenship. He was also refused a reentry visa by the Swiss, and was therefore unable to return to his home in Lausanne until after 1947. Two Léger drawings (£15 each) and a 1916 Gris landscape (£100) were, according to Cooper's personal records, purchased from Reber's wife, Erna.[132] One of the Léger drawings was a detailed study for the oil *Still Life with Bust* (fig. 15), which Cooper had purchased from Léonce Rosenberg in December 1937. This pairing of oil paintings and related drawings was a significant strategy in Cooper's collecting. Recall, for instance, the Gris *Harlequin* and a related drawing (figs. 17, 18) bought at the Zoubaloff auction in 1935, or the Léger drawing *Man and Dog in a Landscape* (fig. 34) purchased from Jeanne Bucher in May 1937 that related to his oil (fig. 16), also from the Zoubaloff collection. Other works Cooper purchased during these years, though bought from other owners, were ultimately from Reber's collection but had been snatched up only shortly before by other collectors and associates.[133] In marked contrast to his pre-war activity, from 1946 through 1950 Cooper made only few, relatively minor purchases.[134]

CONCLUSION

During the war, then, from autumn 1939 through spring 1945, Douglas Cooper's collecting essentially ceased. Over this period, Paris virtually fell from its position as the preeminent art center, and Cooper's first few post-war purchases in 1945 reflect this transfer of art market activity to Switzerland, England, and America. After the war, however, Cooper continued to build his Cubist collection, and he meticulously sought to complete its overall coherence by obtaining major masterpieces and historically key works. However, his collecting would never again approach the pace it took during the years 1933 to 1939. To be sure, financial conditions would simply never again be so advantageous.

There are important conclusions about Cooper's investment that can be drawn from the financial information in this essay. Cooper's purchase prices for 117 works are known; only eleven were unrecorded. He obtained an additional seven works as gifts and two works by trade. He spent a total of £9,023 for 117 works, with £77.1 the average cost per work.

Cooper amassed a formidable collection of about 137 works for approximately £10,000. Adjusted by consumer price indices, this sum would represent about £265,000 today, a relatively small amount that does not account for appreciation of art in today's market. When one examines a few of the prices fetched by a single work over the years, the appreciation of these works becomes dramatically clear: Juan Gris's *Still Life with Guitar on a Table* (1916) was purchased by Cooper in 1939 from G.F. Reber for £300. In 1980, at Sotheby's in London, it fetched £135,000. At Christie's London in 1986 it was bought for £500,000. This last price is about eighty times today's value of what Cooper paid in 1939.[135]

Beyond post-war inflation in the art market, Cooper's investments in art were curtailed because his money was absorbed by the purchase, renovation, and furnishing of the Château de Castille in Argilliers, Gard, in the South of France, where he made his home between 1951 and 1974. Moreover, he commissioned several large-scale works for the château, including Léger's *Trapeze Artists* in 1954 (fig. 38) and the loggia wall, decorated with works based on a series of Picasso drawings and completed in 1962.

After the 1930s Cooper's energy was increasingly absorbed by his activities as an art historian, critic, and curator. In 1949 he published books on Gris, Léger, and Klee. Five years later Cooper's important study of the Courtauld collection was published. Additional publications on Léger and Gris followed in 1956, and a large study of Picasso's variations on Manet's *Déjeuner sur l'herbe* was published in 1962. Cooper's *Picasso-Théâtre* was released in 1967 and the Gris *catalogue raisonné* in 1977. The exhibitions that Cooper organized on Léger (1950 and 1966), on Gris (1956 and 1974), and on Braque (1956 and 1963) culminated in his exhibition catalogues *The Cubist Epoch* (1970) and *The Essential Cubism* (1983).[136] These publications do not even take into account the astonishing number of book reviews, articles, and letters to the editor that Cooper wrote over the years. Indeed, it was after World War II that Cooper, informed by his great collection, emerged as a mature and formidable critic and historian. Cooper's collection of Cubist works of art, however, must be seen essentially as a phenomenon of the 1930s.

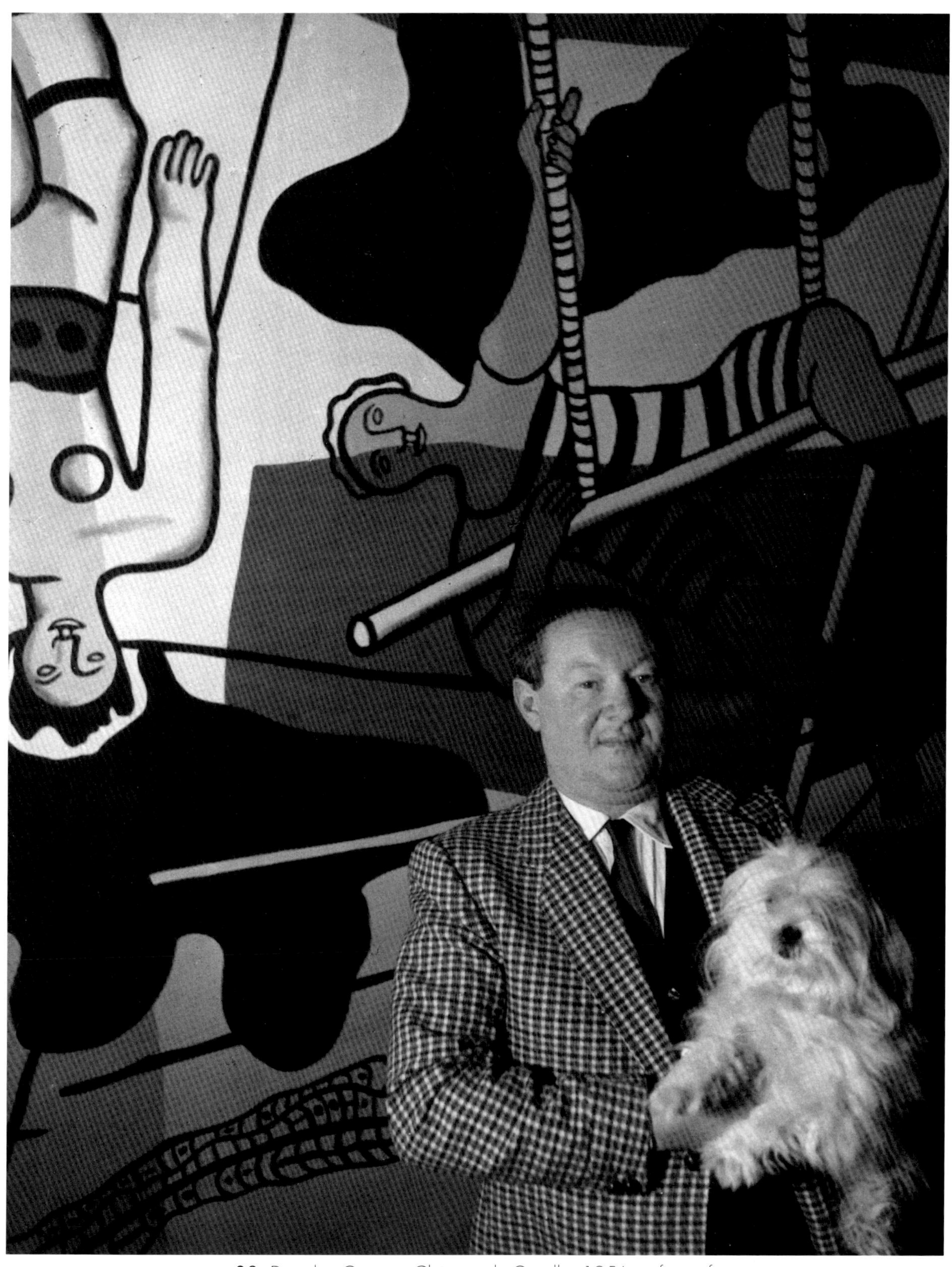

38. Douglas Cooper, Château de Castille, 1956, in front of Fernand Léger's *Trapeze Artists*. (Photo, Robert Doisneau.)

NOTES

DC numbers, which follow titles of works, indicate the inventory numbers in Cooper's own collection records.

Works included in Dorothy Kosinski, *Douglas Cooper und die Meister des Kubismus* (Basel, Kunstmuseum, 1987) are referred to by Kosinski followed by the catalogue number. That publication includes full catalogue information. In all other cases, a selection of the most important or pertinent aspects of provenance, exhibition history, or literature is provided here in order to identify the work and to amplify its context within Cooper's collection, especially its purchase in the 1930s.

Only works from The Douglas Cooper Collection cited in Kosinski include the author's own stick measurements in both inches and centimeters. In all other cases, measurements have been taken from the standard literature or from the lender, and have been converted to centimeters or inches.

Translations are by the author.

Frequently cited abbreviations:

Cooper, *Essential Cubism*:
Douglas Cooper and Gary Tinterow, *The Essential Cubism: Braque, Picasso and Their Friends 1907–1920*, London, The Tate Gallery, 1983.

Cooper, *Gris*:
Douglas Cooper, with the collaboration of Margaret Potter, *Catalogue raisonné de l'oeuvre peint de Juan Gris.* (Paris: Berggruen & Cie, 1977).

Cooper, *Léger*:
Douglas Cooper, *Fernand Léger et le nouvel espace* (Geneva: Editions des Trois Collines, 1949).

Daix:
Pierre Daix and Joan Rosselet, *Le Cubisme de Picasso* (Neuchâtel: Ides et Calendes, 1979).

Dupin, *Miró*:
Jacques Dupin, *Joan Miró, Life and Work* (New York: Abrams, 1962).

Isarlov, *Braque*:
Georges Isarlov, *Georges Braque* (Paris: José Corti, 1932).

Kosinski:
Dorothy Kosinski, *Douglas Cooper und die Meister des Kubismus*, Basel, Kunstmuseum, 1987.

Zervos:
Christian Zervos, *Pablo Picasso* (Paris: Editions Cahiers d'Art, 1932–78), 33 vols.

1 John Richardson, in "Remembering Douglas Cooper," *The New York Review of Books*, April 25, 1985, pp. 24–26, puts Cooper's inheritance at £100,000 and indicates that Cooper earmarked one third of that sum for his collection. However, Cooper's records indicate his expenditure in the 1930s to be in the range of £10,000, with perhaps another £2,000 invested in the Mayor Gallery. In a recent interview with Roderick Coupe, the decorative arts specialist Sir Francis Watson, who knew Cooper already in the 1930s, remembered that with his twenty-first birthday Cooper began to receive a yearly sum of £2,500 from a trust established by his grandmother.

Cooper's acquisitions in the 1930s involved two direct exchanges: Picasso's *Ex Libris Guillaume Apollinaire* (a gift from Alfred Flechtheim in 1935) was traded in April 1939 to Carl Valentin of the Buchholz Gallery, New York, to obtain Klee's 1927 *Fairy Tale* (see note 36, below). Cézanne's *La Préparation du banquet*, purchased from Pierre Loeb in 1933 for £900, was exchanged with Paul Rosenberg in February 1935 for Picasso's 1932 *Still Life with Fruit Dish and Mandolin* (see notes 45 and 51, below, for catalogue details).

2 The prices have been gleaned from collection records kept in Cooper's own hand and, wherever possible, have been confirmed by outside documents. The author thanks Gary Tinterow for providing the information necessary for deciphering Cooper's coded price indications.

3 In addition to the works by Miró and the four Cubists, Cooper's purchases include two works by Paul Klee and one work each by Paul Cézanne, Jean Cocteau, Stanley William Hayter, Henry Moore, and Georges Rouault.

4 The author thanks Mrs. Fred H. Mayor and Mr. James Mayor for their kind assistance and for sharing their ideas and memories, as well as for making available the archival material preserved at the Mayor Gallery. Background information on Mayor is in London, The Mayor Gallery, *A Loan Exhibition in Memory of Fred Hoyland Mayor*, 1973.

5 Among the English artists exhibited by Mayor were Edward Wolfe, Paul Nash, Ivon Hitchens, James Grant, Duncan Grant, Winifred Nicholson, Ben Nicholson, and Michael Sévier. The French artists included Jean Metzinger, Auguste Herbin, Jean Lurçat, Leopold Survage, and Henri Laurens.

6 See P. G. Konody, "Art and Artists," *The Observer*, January 15, 1925, who mentions Herbin, Charles Dufresne, Picasso, and Raoul Dufy; also Konody in *The Observer*, January 24, 1926, concerning the "advanced French art" at Mayor's gallery. Clippings of the articles are in the Douglas Cooper archive, the Getty Study Center for the History of Art and the Humanities, Santa Monica, California.

7 Mayor gave de Maistre a one-person show in 1934. Wolfe had exhibited at the gallery on Sackville Street already in 1925.

8 For more on John Weyman and this close-knit circle of artists and friends, see London, Peter Nahum Gallery, *British Art from the Twentieth Century,* 1989, pp. 20–22, cat. no. 9, where a portrait of Weyman by de Maistre is discussed. According to gallery records, Weyman purchased several works at the Mayor Gallery. In November 1937 Cooper made a gift to him of a 1913 gouache by Léger. De Maistre was a close associate of Francis Bacon, whose furniture designs graced Cooper's home at Groome Place.

9 Other artists who exhibited at the opening of the Mayor Gallery were John Armstrong, Hans Arp, Willi Baumeister, John Bigge, Tristram Hillier, Ludwig Marcoussis, Auguste Herbin, Georges Valmier, and Edward Wadsworth.

10 Paul Nash, letter to the Editor, *The Times* (London), July 2, 1933, from the clipping file preserved in the Cooper archive, Getty Center.

11 This exhibition was a selection of flower still lifes painted by Guillaume, an influential Parisian dealer and collector of avant-garde and tribal art.

12 See Raymond Mortimer, "Cubism," *The New Statesman,* January 9, 1926, concerning the earlier showing of art works from Léonce Rosenberg's gallery and collection. The main sources for the exhibition schedule at the Mayor Gallery are Cooper's scrapbooks in the Cooper archive, Getty Center, as well as the scrapbooks, ledger book, and bills of sale preserved at the Mayor Gallery.

13 *The Scotsman,* November 12, 1936. Clippings of this article and those in the following note are in the Cooper archive, Getty Center.

14 See the *New Statesman and Nation,* December 12, 1936; *The Listener,* February 10, 1937; and *The Daily Express,* June 9, 1937.

15 Other galleries whose importance remains unstudied are the Agnews, Lefèvre, Leicester, New Burlington, Zwemmer, and Redfern Galleries.

16 For the Guggenheim Jeune in London, see the appendix in Angelica Zander Rudenstine, *The Peggy Guggenheim Collection, Venice* (New York: Abrams and the Solomon R. Guggenheim Foundation, 1985), pp. 746–61. Mesens' London Gallery moved to Brook Street in 1947. See correspondence between Mesens and the Museum of Modern Art librarian in the Léger scrapbook, Museum of Modern Art library.

17 Braque, *Still Life with Mandola and Metronome* (DC 1), winter 1909–10, oil on canvas, $31\frac{7}{8} \times 21\frac{5}{16}$ in. (81 × 54.2 cm.); Cooper, *Essential Cubism* no. 10; Isarlov, *Braque* no. 68. Cooper also purchased two works by Picasso from the Zwemmer Gallery. These were *Seated Woman Holding a Book* (DC 40), 1908, ink and watercolor on paper, $19\frac{1}{4} \times 12$ in. (48.9 × 30.5 cm.); Zervos II** no. 722; purchased June 1936 for £60; formerly collection G.F. Reber; and *Head of a Man* (DC 53), 1908(?), watercolor on paper, $12\frac{1}{2} \times 9\frac{3}{4}$ in. (31.8 × 24.8 cm.); Zervos II** no. 716; purchased June 1937 for £35.

18 Douglas Cooper [Douglas Lord], "Cross Sections of English Painting 1938," *The London Bulletin,* July 4–5, 1938, p. 39.

19 The ledger preserved at the Mayor Gallery clearly indicates Kahnweiler's importance as a source of works of art for the gallery.

20 The two paintings were Braque, *Pipe, Apples and Glass* (no DC number), 1933, oil on canvas, $6\frac{1}{4} \times 8\frac{1}{2}$ in. (16 × 22 cm.). Signed l.r.: G. Braque; and *Glass and Apples* (no DC number), 1933, oil on canvas, $9\frac{1}{4} \times 13\frac{1}{2}$ in. (24 × 34 cm.). Signed l.l.: G. Braque. These paintings were resold to the Mayor Gallery in January 1939.

21 In 1936 Cooper bought the following works by Léger: *Landscape* (DC 52), 1913, oil on millboard, 29 × 35 in. (73.7 × 88.9 cm.); illus. Cooper, *Léger* p. 60; *Composition* (DC 11), 1936, oil on canvas, $14\frac{1}{2} \times 17\frac{5}{8}$ in. (36.8 × 44.8 cm.); illus. Caroline Olmes, *Modern Art at Harvard* (New York: Abbeville Press, 1985), p. 68, no. 60; *Composition* (DC 71), 1936, gouache on paper, $12 \times 8\frac{1}{4}$ in. (30.5 × 21 cm.); London, The Tate Gallery, *Fernand Léger,* 1950, no. 59; *Composition* (DC 70), 1936, gouache on paper, $11\frac{1}{4} \times 7\frac{1}{4}$ in. (28.5 × 18 cm.); and *Composition* (DC 21), 1936, gouache on paper, $14\frac{1}{2} \times 9\frac{1}{2}$ in. (36.8 × 24.1 cm.); London, The Tate Gallery, *Fernand Léger,* 1950, no. 60.

22 In 1937 Cooper bought the following Légers from the artist: *The Blue Cock* (DC 69), 1937, gouache on paper, $12\frac{1}{2} \times 14\frac{3}{4}$ in. (31.8 × 37.5 cm.); illus. Cooper, *Léger* p. 131; *The Red Cock* (DC 68), 1937, gouache on paper, $12\frac{3}{4} \times 14\frac{1}{2}$ in. (32.4 × 36.8 cm.); *Composition—Butterflies and Flower* (DC 77), 1937, gouache on paper, $14\frac{1}{4} \times 10$ in. (36.5 × 26 cm.); London, The Tate Gallery, *Fernand Léger,* 1950, no. 61; Sotheby Parke Bernet, London, *Important Impressionist and Modern Drawings and Watercolours,* June 29, 1977, lot 238; and *Composition* (DC 78), 1937, gouache on paper, $12\frac{1}{2} \times 9\frac{1}{2}$ in. (32 × 24.5 cm.); exh. London, The Tate Gallery, *Fernand Léger,* 1950 (not in catalogue).

23 The group of seven related Léger drawings purchased in 1939 included *Woman's Head* (DC 179), 1939, ink on paper, $15\frac{1}{2} \times 12\frac{1}{2}$ in. (39.4 × 31.8 cm.); London, The Tate Gallery, *Fernand Léger,* 1950, no. 65; illus. Cooper, *Léger* p. 134; *Woman's Head and Leg* (DC 175), 1939, ink on paper, $15\frac{1}{2} \times 12\frac{1}{2}$ in. (39.4 × 31.8 cm.); London, The Tate Gallery, *Fernand Léger,* 1950, no. 64; *The Hands* (DC 176), 1939, ink on paper, $16 \times 12\frac{1}{2}$ in. (40.6 × 31.8 cm.); London, The Tate Gallery, *Fernand Léger,* 1950, no. 63; illus. Cooper, *Léger* p. 135; *Two Heads* (DC 177), 1939, ink on paper, $15\frac{1}{2} \times 12\frac{1}{2}$ in. (39.4 × 31.8 cm.); London, The Tate Gallery, *Fernand Léger,* 1950, no. 62; *Head of a Woman* (DC 178), 1939, ink on paper, $15\frac{3}{8} \times 12\frac{5}{8}$ in. (39.4 × 31.8 cm.); London, The Tate Gallery, *Fernand Léger,* 1950, no. 66; *Woman's Head and Hand* (no DC number),

1939, ink on paper; illus. Cooper, *Léger* p. 106; and *Woman with Hand before Face* (no DC number), 1939, ink on paper, 15⅜ × 12⅝ in. (39.1 × 32.1 cm.). At one point, this work was part of Basil Amulree's collection.

In 1934 Léger gave Cooper a gift of his *Composition* (DC 19), 1934, gouache on paper, 11 × 15½ in. (27.9 × 39.4 cm.). Cooper received other gifts from artists, including, in 1933, Jean Cocteau's *Self-Portrait* (DC 250), 1926, ink on paper, 12 × 9¾ in. (30.5 × 24.8 cm.). Inscribed: Maison de Santé de Thermes/très cordial souvenir à D.F. Cooper. Also in 1934, Miró gave Cooper his *Programme, Ballets Russes de Monte-Carlo, New York* (DC 48), 1933–34, gouache maquette, 12½ × 9 13/16 in. (31.8 × 25 cm.); Kosinski no. 49. Works that Cooper purchased directly from artists included Henry Moore, *Drawing for a Sculpture*, 1932, see note 44, below; Picasso, *Portrait of Dora Maar* (DC 106), April 27, 1938, pastel on paper, 30 × 22 in. (76 × 56 cm.), which he purchased in November 1938 for £60; and Rouault, *Head of a Woman* (DC 47), oil on paper, 10½ × 8 in. (27 × 20.5 cm.), which Cooper purchased in 1935 for £12.

24 Gris, *Glass and Bottle* (DC 96), 1919, oil on canvas, 18⅛ × 10⅝ in. (46 × 27 cm.); Cooper, *Gris* no. 95. The *catalogue raisonné* indicates that it was purchased from Ronald Fleming. This discrepancy indicates, once again, the tangled affairs between Cooper and the Mayor Gallery.

25 Braque, *Landscape at La Ciotat* (DC 105), 1907, oil on canvas, 28¼ × 23⅜ in. (71.8 × 59.4 cm.); Isarlov, *Braque* no. 24; New York, The Museum of Modern Art, *Picasso and Braque: Pioneering Cubism*, 1989, p. 77.

26 The two drawings by Gris were *Fruit Bowl and Glass* (DC 108), 1923, charcoal on paper, 7½ × 11 in. (18.5 × 28 cm.); Juan Antonio Gaya-Nuños, *Juan Gris* (Boston: New York Graphic Society, 1975), illus. 425; and *Still Life with Guitar and Sheet Music* (DC 111), 1923, ink and gouache on paper, 9⅞ × 12⅛ in. (24 × 30.8 cm.); Kosinski no. 20.

27 See Pierre Assouline, *L'Homme de l'art, D.-H. Kahnweiler* (Paris: Balland, 1988), pp. 329–31. Additional correspondence preserved at the Galerie Louise Leiris has yet to be consulted by this author.

28 The three works by Gris were *Carafe and Glass* (DC 51), 1919, oil on canvas, 16 × 13 in. (41 × 33 cm.); Cooper, *Gris* no. 300; purchased for £35; *Still Life: Guitar and Set-Square* (DC 49), 1926, oil on canvas, 26 × 33 in. (66 × 84 cm.); Cooper, *Gris* no. 582; purchased for £175; and *Guitar and Fruit Dish* (DC 2), 1921, oil on canvas, 19⅝ × 24 in. (50 × 61 cm.); Cooper, *Gris* no. 374; purchased for £80. Cooper traded this work back to Kahnweiler's Galerie Simon in 1937 as part of his purchase of the 1917 painting *Harlequin*.

29 Léger, *Contraste de formes* (DC 13), 1913, oil on canvas, 21⅜ × 18½ in. (55 × 46 cm.); Paris, Galerie Berggruen, *Léger, Contrastes de formes*, 1962.

30 Gris, *Harlequin* (DC 55), 1917, oil on canvas, 28¾ × 21¼ in. (73 × 54 cm.); Cooper, *Gris* no. 242; purchased for £100; and Gris, *Guitar and Fruit Dish*, 1921, see note 28, above.

31 Picasso, *Still Life with Peaches and Playing Cards* (DC 89), 1914, pencil and watercolor, 19 × 24½ in. (48.3 × 62.3 cm.); Kosinski no. 62.

32 The three early Léger nudes were *Reclining Nude* (DC 102), 1907(?), ink on paper, 12½ × 9½ in. (32 × 24 cm.); London, The Tate Gallery, *Fernand Léger*, 1950, no. 47; *Standing Nude* (DC 101), 1911, ink on paper, 12⅞ × 9 5/16 in. (32.6 × 23.7 cm.); illus. Cooper, *Léger* p. 39; Kosinski no. 28; and *Male Nude Seen from Behind* (DC 112), 1911, ink on paper, 9½ × 13 in. (24 × 33 cm.); illus. Cooper, *Léger* p. 39.

33 The most comprehensive presentation of Flechtheim's life and career is *Alfred Flechtheim: Sammler, Kunsthändler, Verleger* (Düsseldorf: Kunstmuseum, 1987).

34 Picasso, *Still Life with Dead Birds* (DC 34), summer 1912, oil on canvas, 18⅛ × 25⅝ in. (46 × 65 cm.). Signed on reverse: Picasso, Sorgues 1912. Zervos II* no. 339; Daix no. 494. This work was included in several important exhibitions during the 1930s: London, Reid & Lefèvre, *Thirty Years of Picasso*, 1931, no. 11; Paris, Galerie Georges Petit, *Exposition Picasso*, 1932, no. 77; Zurich, Kunsthaus, *Picasso*, 1932, no. 63; London, Mayor Gallery, *20th Century Classics*, 1934, no. 6. Cooper included the work in: Dallas, Museum of Fine Arts, *Picasso*, 1967, no. 21.

35 Picasso, *The Soldier* (DC 45), c. 1901, crayon on paper, 6 × 4½ in. (15.2 × 11.4 cm.). Signed u.l.: Picasso; l.r.: Vive la Classe.

36 Picasso, *Ex Libris Guillaume Apollinaire* (DC 39), 1905, watercolor and ink on paper, 7½ × 4½ in. (19 × 12 cm.). Signed l.r.: Picasso fecit. See note 1, above, concerning the trade to Curt Valentin in May 1939, confirmed in a letter from Valentin to Cooper, May 9, 1939, in the Valentin archive at the library of the Museum of Modern Art, New York. In that trade, Cooper received Klee's *Fairy Tale* for which he paid an additional $220. Valentin subsequently sold the Picasso to Walter Chrysler.

37 Picasso, *Head of a Woman* (DC 41), 1909, ink and charcoal on paper, 24½ × 18¼ in. (62.2 × 46.4 cm.). Signed on verso. Zervos II** no. 713; exhibited Mayor Gallery, 1934, no. 2.

38 Gris, *Still Life with Fruit Dish and Guitar* (DC 8), 1925, pen and brush and black ink heightened with white on paper, 11 × 8½ in. (28 × 21.5 cm.). Signed l.c.: Juan Gris. D.-H. Kahnweiler, *Juan Gris: His Life, His Work*, trans. D. Cooper (New York, 1947), p. 55, no. 24.

39 Klee's work had been exhibited at least ten times in

Flechtheim's galleries between 1919 and 1932. See Düsseldorf, Kunstmuseum, *Alfred Flechtheim,* p. 266. Flechtheim may have actually been the source of Kahnweiler's business relationship with Klee. In December 1935, Kahnweiler wrote to Flechtheim asking him to speak to Freddy Mayor concerning the dissolution of the commission system with which they had all been working. Suffering from the economic situation, Kahnweiler explained the pressing need to withdraw this financial support from Flechtheim. He cited somewhat defensively that he had given over half of the Klee profits to Flechtheim, even though it had been Hermann Rupf's suggestion that had brought Klee to work with Kahnweiler. Cited in *Alfred Flechtheim,* p. 207; the correspondence is in the Galerie Louise Leiris archives. In the same catalogue, see also Stefan Frey and Wolfgang Kersten, "Paul Klees geschäftliche Verbindung zur Galerie Alfred Flechtheim," pp. 64–91, especially pp. 90–91 concerning the Mayor Gallery exhibition in 1934 and Kahnweiler's subsequent contract with Klee, dated February 10 of that year. See also notes 208, 220, and 243 citing correspondence between Kahnweiler and Hermann Rupf, including references to the business arrangements between himself and Flechtheim: "Flechtheim is giving me all the Klees he has, and will, with the agreement of Klee, have a part of any sales (Flechtheim gibt mir alle Klees, die er hatte, und wird von mir, mit Einverständnis von Klee, an dem Geschaefte beteiligt)"; see also p. 207 concerning Flechtheim's 20% commission. In the same catalogue, see Cordula Frowein, "Alfred Flechtheim im Exil in England," pp. 58–63, including a *pro forma* contract letter dated April 3, 1934 (apparently back dated, and issued in November or December of that year) that outlines in the most general terms the arrangement between the Galerie Simon, the Mayor Gallery, and Alfred Flechtheim, an arrangement which evolved out of their discussions in Paris in the autumn of the previous year.

40 Klee, *Barockbildnis* (DC 9), listed by Cooper as *Portrait of an Artist,* was no. 21 in London, Mayor Gallery, *20th Century Classics,* in February 1934. See New York, Museum of Modern Art, *Paul Klee,* ed. Carolyn Lanchner, 1987, illus. p. 154.

41 See letters to Klee dated January 20 and March 6, 1934 and February 22 and May 7, 1935, preserved with the Klee Bequest, Bern. Correspondence from the artist in Bern to the gallery, dated December 12, 1934, accepts £15 for *Approaching Snowstorm (Drohender Schneesturm), Hovering (Schwebendes), The Fleeing Spirit (Der fliehende Geist), Fruit (Die Frucht),* and *Happy Mountain Landscape (Heitere gebirgs Landschaft).*

Klee also requested the pictures for the exhibition *Paul Klee* at the Bern Kunsthalle, held February 23 to March 24, 1935. This exhibition was also shown at the Basel Kunsthalle, October 27 to November 24, 1935.

Fruit and *Approaching Snowstorm* had been included in the 1934 exhibition in London, according to a review in *The Times,* January 1934, rpt. in Monika Flacke-Knoch and Stephan von Weise, "Der Lebensfilm von Alfred Flechtheim," in *Alfred Flechtheim,* p. 200.

In a letter preserved in the Cooper archive, Getty Center, Klee acknowledged previous correspondence from the Mayor Gallery, extended thanks for Alfred Flechtheim's greetings, and begged for more direct correspondence from him.

42 Léger, *Man and Dog in a Landscape (Paysage animé, l'Homme au chien),* 1921, oil on canvas, 18 × 25 in. (45.5 × 65.5 cm.); Basel, Galerie Beyeler, *Fernand Léger,* 1981, no. 15. The next year, at the November 1935 sale of the collection of Jacques Zoubaloff, Cooper obviously sought to replace this Léger with a similar composition, for he purchased lot no. 149, *Man with Dog in a Landscape (Paysage animé, l'Homme au chien),* 1921, see note 59, below.

43 For the legal difficulties and lack of written confirmations that bedeviled the two dealers' shared enterprises, see Pierre Assouline, *L'Homme de l'art, D.-H. Kahnweiler,* pp. 336–37.

44 See note 23, above, for the Cocteau self-portrait. The Moore was *Drawing for a Sculpture* (DC 32), 1933, ink and wash on paper, 21½ × 14½ in. (54.6 × 36.8 cm.). Signed l.r.: Moore 33. It had been exhibited at the Leicester Gallery in the 1933 Moore exhibition. Herbert Read, *Henry Moore* (London, 1944). It was resold to Leicester Gallery in May 1951. See Kosinski no. 54 for complete catalogue information for Picasso, *Head of a Woman, Casket and Apple,* 1909.

45 Cézanne, *La Préparation du banquet,* c. 1890, oil on canvas, 17¾ × 21¼ in. (45 × 54 cm.). Now in a private collection, Japan, the work is no. 586 in Lionello Venturi, *Cézanne: Son art — son oeuvre* (Paris: Paul Rosenberg, 1936), 2 vols. See Mary Louise Krumrine, *Die Badenden,* Basel Kunstmuseum, 1989, illus. 24.

46 This was Léger's *Composition,* 1934, see note 23, above. A letter from Léger in Paris to Simone Herman, dated January 9, 1935, describes his previous evening at the restaurant Boeuf sur le toit: "Night on the town with Flechtheim — Cooper — de Maré — three pederasts — Boeuf sur le toit — champagne — very nice evening...(Saoulerie avec Flechtheim — Cooper — de Maré — trois pédérastes — Boeuf sur le toit — champagne — soirée très gentille...)." See Fernand Léger, *Lettres à Simone* (Lausanne: Skira for Centre Georges Pompidou, Musée National d'Art Moderne, 1987), p. 133.

47 Stanley William Hayter, *Reclining Woman* (DC 64), 1934, engraving, 11½ × 14½ in. (29 × 37 cm.); edition 1/50. Signed l.r.: S.W. Hayter, 1934. Given to the Print Room of the British Museum, December 1954.

48 Miró, *Composition* (DC 48), 1933, gouache on paper, 18½ x 25 in. (47 × 63.5 cm.). Signed, verso: Joan Miró, 1933. Dupin, *Miró* no. 309, p. 509. Exhibited: London, Zwemmer Gallery, May 1937, no. 15. Subsequently sold to Klaus Perls. Correspondence from Miró dated March 9, 1935 requests payment and confirms the work was

purchased in summer 1934. The letter established the purchase price at Fr. 700, and Cooper's collection card for this object indicates £10.

49 Correspondence from Miró to Cooper dated January 2, 1934, in the Cooper archive, Getty Center, indicates that an exhibition at Pierre Matisse Gallery in New York coincided with the peformances of the Ballets Russes there. For the maquette, see note 23, above, and Kosinski no. 49.

50 These two Picasso still lifes were *Guitar on a Table* (DC 44), 1920, gouache on paper, $8\frac{1}{2} \times 7\frac{1}{2}$ in. (21.6 × 19 cm.). Signed u.l.: Picasso. Dated on reverse. Purchased for Fr. 12, sold June 1946 to Georges Maratier, Galerie Allard, Paris; and *The Artist's Table* (DC 46), 1920, charcoal on paper, $11 \times 8\frac{1}{2}$ in. (27.9 × 21.6 cm.). Signed u.l.: Picasso 11–20. Purchased for £10; see Zervos VI no. 1414.

51 Picasso, *Still Life with Fruit Dish and Mandolin* (DC 33), 1932, oil on canvas, $38\frac{1}{4} \times 51\frac{3}{16}$ in. (96.8 × 129.9 cm.). Signed l.r.: Picasso 13.2.32. Zervos VII no. 375; illus. *Cahiers d'Art,* 1932, p. 147. During the 1930s the work was included in the following important exhibitions. Exhibited: Paris, Galerie Georges Petit, *Exposition Picasso,* 1932, no. 213; Zurich, Kunsthaus, *Picasso,* September 1932, no. 214. Cooper included the work in: Marseilles, Musée Cantini, *Picasso,* 1959, no. 38.

52 In fact, this exhibition was not devoted exclusively to Léger but included many of the "lesser" Cubists. The exhibition may have been the one to which Kahnweiler objected so strongly on the grounds that it obscured the importance of the "true" Cubists. See Assouline, *L'Homme de l'art, D.-H. Kahnweiler,* p. 331 and note 27, above.

53 Léger, *Still Life with a Book* (DC 86), 1914, oil on canvas, $36\frac{1}{4} \times 28\frac{3}{4}$ in. (92 × 73 cm.). Signed verso: Nature Morte, F. Léger, '14. Illus. Cooper, *Léger* p. 57. Exhibited: Paris, Petit Palais, *Maîtres de l'Art Indépendant,* June 1937; London, The Tate Gallery, *Fernand Léger,* 1950, no. 11.

54 The two versions were *Two Reclining Women* (*Deux femmes couchées,* no DC number), 1913, gouache and wash on paper, $19\frac{3}{4} \times 25\frac{5}{8}$ in. (50.2 × 65.1 cm.). Signed and inscribed: FL. '13 Deux femmes couchées. Exhibited at New York, Saidenberg Gallery, *Fernand Léger, Gouaches, Watercolors and Drawings,* 1910–53, 1968, no. 4. Sold at Sotheby's London, *Impressionist and Modern Drawings, Paintings and Sculpture,* April 24, 1968, lot 135; sold at Christie's New York, *Impressionist and Modern Paintings and Sculpture (Part I)* May 15, 1990, lot 43; and *Two Reclining Women* (DC 14), 1913, gouache and oil on paper, $25 \times 19\frac{1}{2}$ in. (63.5 × 49.5 cm.). Signed l.r.: F.L. 13/deux femmes couchées. Cooper, *Léger* p. 59.

55 These three works by Léger were Study for *Woman in Red and Green* (DC 17), 1913, gouache and ink on paper, $25\frac{5}{8} \times 19\frac{5}{8}$ in. (65 × 50 cm.). Signed l.r.: FL 13; and l.l.: dessin pour la femme en rouge et vert. Exhibited: Zurich, 1933, no. 64; Paris, Musée National d'Art Moderne, Centre Georges Pompidou, *Donation Louise et Michel Leiris,* 1984, no. 104, illus. p. 118. Cooper's collection card notes: "Given to Léger in December 1954 in exchange for *Les Trapézistes* on my staircase"; *Still Life* (DC 18), 1913, gouache and oil on paper, $18\frac{7}{8} \times 23\frac{3}{8}$ in. (47.7 × 59.3 cm.); Kosinski no. 30, illus. p. 106; and Study for *Le Balcon* (DC 20), 1913, gouache on paper, $25 \times 19\frac{1}{4}$ in. (63.5 × 48.9 cm.). Signed and inscribed l.r.: FL 13, Nature Morte dessin pour le balcon. Illus. Cooper, *Léger* p. 55. Cooper's collection card notes: "Exchanged with Berggruen, April 1958 for Braque no. 308."

56 The December 1937 purchases of Léger works from Rosenberg were Drawing for *The Cardplayers* (DC 87), 1916–17, wash and pencil on paper, $20\frac{3}{4} \times 14\frac{7}{8}$ in. (52.7 × 37.8 cm.); Kosinski no. 33; illus. Cooper, *Léger* p. 66; Drawing for *The Cardplayers* (DC 91), 1916–17, double-sided wash drawing on paper, $20\frac{1}{2} \times 14\frac{5}{8}$ in. (52 × 37.5 cm.). Recto signed and inscribed l.r.: dessin pour "La Partie de cartes" [fragment] F. Léger; verso signed l.r.: F.L. 17. According to Cooper's collection card, the work was exchanged with Eugene Thaw of New York, who subsequently had the paper divided to separate the two drawings. The recto was exhibited in Houston at Janie C. Lee Gallery, *Cubist Drawings, 1907–1929,* 1983, no. 30; *Composition: Man in a Factory* (DC 82), 1920, watercolor on paper, $22 \times 16\frac{1}{2}$ in. (56 × 42 cm.). Signed l.r.: FL 20. Now collection of Galerie Krugier & Geofroy, Geneva. Cooper's records indicate the sale of the work to Heinz Berggruen in 1977; and *Still Life with Bust* (DC 81), 1924, oil on canvas, $25\frac{1}{2} \times 19\frac{5}{8}$ in. (64.6 × 49.7 cm.); purchased for £15. Recto signed l.r.: F. Léger; verso signed: Nature Morte/F. Léger. Rosenberg stock no. 8380. Illus. Cooper, *Léger* p. 100; London, The Tate Gallery, *Fernand Léger,* 1950, no. 25. In 1945 Cooper purchased the preparatory drawing for this picture from Mrs. Erna Reber, Lausanne; see Kosinski no. 41.

57 The Zoubaloff sale was held on November 27 and 28, 1935. This followed an earlier auction of Zoubaloff's collection, held June 16 and 17, 1927, which included works by Auguste Rodin, Aristide Maillol, Pierre Auguste Renoir, Paul Cézanne, Odilon Redon, and Constantin Guys. There also seems to have been a dispersal of material from the Zoubaloff Collection during the previous year. See *Beaux Arts,* December 6, 1935, p. 4; *Gazette de l'Hôtel Drouot,* November 30, 1935, p. 1; and *Gazette de l'Hôtel Drouot,* November 28, 1935, p. 2.

58 Other artists represented in the sale include Albert Gleizes, August Herbin, Henri Laurens, Léger, André Lhote, Jean Lurçat, Ludwig Marcoussis, Leopold Survage, and Georges Valmier. The sale realized Fr. 210,000.

59 Cooper bid Fr. 2,150 for lot 149, Léger, *Man with Dog in a Landscape* (DC 109), 1921, oil on canvas, $25\frac{1}{2} \times 36$ in. (64.8 × 91.4 cm.). Recto signed l.r.: F. Léger. Provenance: Galerie Simon, Paris; Jacques Zoubaloff, sale November 1935, Hôtel Drouot,

Paris, no. 149. Exhibited: London, The Tate Gallery, *Fernand Léger,* 1950, no. 20; Berlin, Staatliche Kunsthalle, *Fernand Léger, 1881–1935,* 1980–81, no. 31, illus. color p. 209; New York, Acquavella Gallery, *Fernand Léger,* 1987, no. 27, illus. color.

60 Cooper bid Fr. 8,100 for lot 130, Gris, *Seated Harlequin with Guitar* (DC 4), 1919, oil on canvas, 45⅝ × 35 in. (116 × 89 cm.). Signed l.l.: Juan Gris/10–1. Provenance: formerly Léonce Rosenberg, Galerie de l'Effort Moderne; Jacques Zoubaloff, sale Hôtel Drouot, Paris, November 18–27, 1935, no. 130; December 1938, sold by Cooper to Galerie Beaune; Georges Maratier(?); currently, Donation Leiris, Musée de l'Art Moderne, Centre Georges Pompidou, Paris; Cooper, *Gris* no. 321.

61 Cooper bid Fr. 2,300 for Picasso, *Nature morte,* 1922, oil on canvas, 6⅞ × 9⅛ in. (16 × 22 cm.). Signed l.r.: Picasso. Provenance: Douglas Cooper, The Mayor Gallery (Mayor Gallery no. 1848); to A.E. Gallatin, June 13, 1936 (the Mayor Gallery invoice, in Cooper's handwriting, indicates the selling price of £40 — this reflected £25 to Cooper himself and £15 profit to Mayor Gallery); A.E. Gallatin Collection, The Philadelphia Museum of Art. Zervos IV no. 413; Guillaume Janneau, *L'Art cubiste* (Paris: Editions d'Art Charles Moreau, 1929), pl. 43.

62 Cooper's bids on Gris works were Lot 30, for Fr. 1,000, *Harlequin with a Guitar* (*La Guitariste,* DC 127), 1922, gouache on paper, 9½ × 5¾ in. (24 × 14.5 cm.). Signed l.l.: Juan Gris, 1922. Provenance: Galerie Simon, Paris; Jacques Zoubaloff, sale Paris, Hôtel Drouot, 1935, no. 30; stolen from Cooper 1974; Cooper, *Gris,* no. 396a; Lot 31, for Fr. 250, *Still Life with Guitar, Book, and Newspaper* (*Etude,* DC 6), 1920, pencil on paper, 11¾ × 9 in. (26 × 21 cm.). Provenance: Léonce Rosenberg (photo no. 184; stock no. 6661); Jacques Zoubaloff, sale Paris, Hôtel Drouot, November 1935, no. 31; sold to Lionel Préjger, Paris, 1977; Lot 32, for Fr. 400, Drawing for *Seated Harlequin with Guitar* (DC 55), 1919, pencil on paper, 13⁵⁄₁₆ × 9¹⁵⁄₁₆ in. (33.8 × 25.2 cm.). Signed l.l.: Juan Gris, 1919. Provenance: Léonce Rosenberg; Jacques Zoubaloff, sale Hôtel Drouot, Paris, 1935, no. 32; subsequently sold to Lionel Préjger, Paris, 1977; and Lot 36, for Fr. 410, *Still Life with Cup and Glass* (DC 50), 1911, pencil on paper, 14¹⁄₁₆ × 12⅝ in. (35.7 × 32 cm.); Kosinski no. 13.

63 Research has not revealed more of her identity; however, according to entry no. 74 in Cooper, *Essential Cubism,* Mlle. Pertuisot was later Mrs. Gerard Lee Bevan, London.

64 Gris, *Portrait of Josette Gris* (DC 84), 1916, oil on panel, 45½ × 28¾ in. (116 × 73 cm.); Pertuisot sale lot 39; Cooper, *Gris* no. 203; Cooper, *Essential Cubism* no. 74; bequeathed to the Museo del Prado in 1977. Douglas Cooper's record indicates £165, however the auction records indicate £173 5s. Gris, *Still Life with Mandolin* (DC 85), 1919, oil on canvas, 36¼ × 25¾ in. (92 × 65 cm.); Pertuisot sale lot 41; Cooper, *Gris* no. 303. Douglas Cooper's record indicates £120, as does the auction record. Picasso, *Abstraction* (no DC number), 1922, oil on canvas, 12½ × 15¾ in. (31.8 × 40 cm.); Pertuisot sale lot 59. According to auction records, the amount paid was £78. Miró, *A Bather on the Seashore* (no DC number), 1926, charcoal and watercolor on paper, 24½ × 18 in. (62.2 × 45.7 cm.); Pertuisot sale lot 26. This work was listed in Cooper's records as *Woman Chasing a Bird,* 1928, pencil and watercolor. According to auction records, Cooper paid £6; there is no price indication in his own records.

65 Other successful bidders included Arthur Tooth & Cie., Zwemmer, Edwardes, Knoedler, Paul Rosenberg, Reid & Lefèvre, Rosenberg & Helft, and D.-H. Kahnweiler.

66 For Earl Horter, see Anne d'Harnoncourt, "A.E. Gallatin and the Arensbergs: Pioneer Collectors of Twentieth-Century Art," *Apollo* 99 (July 1974), pp. 52–61.

67 Undated correspondence from Horter in the Cooper archive, Getty Center.

68 Undated correspondence from Horter in the Cooper archive, Getty Center.

69 Undated correspondence from Horter in the Cooper archive, Getty Center.

70 Horter clearly regretted the sale of his pictures. Other works he owned include Picasso, *Standing Female Nude,* 1910, oil on canvas; Zervos II* no. 194; now in the Albright Knox Art Gallery, Buffalo; and Picasso, *Portrait of a Woman,* 1910; Zervos II* no. 234; now in the Museum of Fine Arts, Boston.

71 The three 1937 purchases from Horter were Braque, *Still Life with Glass and Newspaper* (DC 58), summer 1913, oil and charcoal on oval canvas, 38¾ × 28 in. (98.4 × 71.1 cm.). Signed l.r.: G. Braque, signed verso (lined): G. Braque/Sorgues. Currently collection Heinz Berggruen, Geneva. Isarlov, *Braque,* no. 165, pl. 19; Geneva, Musée d'art et d'histoire, *Berggruen Collection,* 1988, no. 30, illus. p. 87; Picasso, *Nude* (DC 36), 1909, oil on canvas, 35¼ × 28 in. (89.5 × 71.1 cm.); subsequently Morton G. Neumann Family Collection; Zervos II* no. 176; and Picasso, *Still Life with Bottle, Cup and Newspaper* (DC 54), 1912–13, *papier collé,* charcoal, and oil on paper, 24 × 18½ in. (63 × 48 cm.). Signed verso: Picasso. Museum Folkwang, Essen; Zervos II** no. 397; Daix, no. 545; Bielefeld, Kunsthalle, *Zeichnungen und Collagen des Kubismus: Picasso, Braque, Gris,* 1979, no. 87, as collection Kunstsammlung Nordrhein-Westfalen Düsseldorf.

72 Reber, a German born in Oerlinghausen, near Bielefeld, had lived in Switzerland (in Lucerne, Ascona, Lugano, and finally Lausanne) since 1919. The author's forthcoming article in *Burlington Magazine* presents a complete picture of Reber, his collection, and his impact on Cooper.

73 See note 132, below, for catalogue information concerning the two works on paper by Léger and the oil by Gris that Cooper purchased from Reber's wife, Erna, in the 1940s.

74 See Berlin, Galerie Alfred Flechtheim, *Pablo Picasso*, 1927.

75 Braque, *Still Life with a Guitar* (DC 66), 1924, oil on canvas, $46\frac{1}{2} \times 24$ in. (118.1×61 cm.); the Jacques and Natasha Gelman Collection. Signed l.l.: G. Braque '24. Illus. Carl Einstein, *Braque* (Paris: Chroniques du Jour, 1934), pl. 60; Isarlov, *Braque* no. 331, p. 24. Included in the following exhibitions in the 1920s and 1930s: Paris, Paul Rosenberg, *Braque*, 1926, no. 45; Basel, Kunsthalle, *Georges Braque*, 1933, no. 112; London, The Tate Gallery, 1938. Subsequently Cooper included it in the following exhibitions: London, The Tate Gallery, *Georges Braque*, 1956, no. 54, pl. 22G; Munich, Haus der Kunst, *Georges Braque*, 1963, no. 60, illus. 63; The Art Institute of Chicago, *Braque: The Great Years*, 1972, no. 7, fig. 36.

Gris, *Still Life with Guitar on a Table* (DC 126), 1916, oil on canvas, $36\frac{3}{16} \times 23\frac{3}{8}$ in. (92×59.3 cm.). Signed l.l.: Juan Gris 1–16. *Cahiers d'Art* 1933, nos. 5–6, illus. p. 200; Cooper, *Gris* no. 158; Cooper, *Juan Gris ou le goût du solonnel*, Geneva, 1949, pl. 8. Exhibited: Baden-Baden, Staatliche Kunsthalle, *Juan Gris*, 1974, no. 37, illus.; Madrid, Sala Pablo Picasso, *Juan Gris*, 1985, no. 44, illus. p. 195.

76 Picasso, *Standing Female Nude* (DC 141), 1906–07, black ink and red gouache with wash on paper, $24\frac{1}{4} \times 16\frac{11}{16}$ in. (61.5×42.4 cm.); Kosinski no. 50; see brief discussion p. 136 and notes 141–43.

77 Regarding the relationship with Cézanne, note for example Cézanne's *Trois baigneuses*, 1875–77, oil on canvas; no. 267 in Lionello Venturi, *Cézanne: Son art — son oeuvre* (Paris: Paul Rosenberg, 1936), 2 vols; illus. *Die Badenden*, Basel, Kunstmuseum, 1989, p. 145, fig. 108. See especially Christian Geelhaar's essay, "Die richtigen Augen der Maler," in particular p. 292 ff., concerning Picasso's appreciation of Cézanne's bathers.

78 Picasso, *Three Figures under a Tree*, winter 1907–08, oil on canvas, 39×39 in. (99×99 cm.). Signed u.r.: Picasso. Gift to Etat Français for Musée Picasso, Paris, 1976. Zervos II* no. 53; Daix no. 106. It was included in the following exhibitions in the 1930s: Vienna, Kunstlerhaus, Gesellschaft zur Förderung Moderner Kunst in Wien, *Die Kunst in unserer Zeit: Moderne französische Kunst*, 1930; Paris, Galerie Georges Petit, *Exposition Picasso*, 1932, no. 51; Kunsthaus Zürich, *Picasso*, 1932, no. 41. Cooper included it in: Marseilles, Musée Cantini, *Picasso*, 1959, no. 9; Cooper, *Essential Cubism* no. 113.

79 Picasso, *Nude Woman in an Armchair* (DC 65), summer 1909, oil on canvas, $36\frac{1}{2} \times 29\frac{1}{2}$ in. (93.5×75 cm.); Zervos II* no. 174. It was in the following important exhibitions of the 1930s: Paris, Galeries Georges Petit, *Exposition Picasso*, 1932, no. 59 (catalogue by Charles Vrancken); Kunsthaus Zürich, *Picasso*, 1932, no. 53, pl. VII (catalogue by C. Vrancken and W. Wartmann). Later, Cooper included it in the following exhibitions: Marseilles, Musée Cantini, *Picasso*, 1959, no. 15, illus. frontispiece; The Los Angeles County Museum of Art and New York, Metropolitan Museum, *The Cubist Epoch*, 1970–71, no. 231, pl. 14; Cooper, *Essential Cubism*, no. 118.

80 Picasso, *The Clarinet Player* (DC 59), 1911/12, oil on canvas, $42\frac{15}{16} \times 27\frac{1}{8}$ in. (109×69 cm.); Zervos II* no. 288. During the 1930s it was exhibited in Paris, Galeries Georges Petit, *Exposition Picasso*, 1932, no. 80; Kunsthaus Zürich, *Picasso*, 1932, no. 68. Cooper also included it in Marseilles, Musée Cantini, *Picasso*, 1959, no. 18.

Picasso, *Bottle of "Bass" and Guitar* (no DC number), 1912–13, pastel, charcoal, and stenciled black ink on Ingres paper, $18\frac{3}{4} \times 25$ in. (47.7×63.5 cm.). Signed verso u.l. in pencil: Picasso. Zervos II** no. 376; Cooper, *Essential Cubism* no. 169; Kosinski no. 60.

81 See Kosinski, p. 144.

82 Picasso, *Two Women* (DC 110), 1920, pastel on paper, $24 \times 18\frac{1}{2}$ in. (61×47 cm.); stolen from the Château de Castille in 1974; Zervos IV no. 56; and Picasso, *Head of a Woman* (DC 132), 1921, oil on canvas, $8\frac{5}{8} \times 6\frac{3}{8}$ in. (22.5×16 cm.); stolen from the Château de Castille in 1974; Zervos IV no. 357. Other related works in Reber's collection were *Two Nude Women*, 1920, pencil and gouache on paper, Zervos IV no. 63; *Women*, 1920–21, pastel(?); Zervos IV no. 217; *Woman Drying Her Feet*, 1921, pastel on paper, Zervos IV no. 330; *Mother and Child*, 1921, pencil on paper, Zervos IV no. 235; *Head of a Woman*, 1921, pastel on paper, Zervos IV no. 356; *Woman with Drapery*, 1922, sanguine on paper, Zervos V no. 172; *Mother and Child*, 1922, oil on canvas, Zervos IV no. 371; and *Seated Nude, Left Arm Resting on Rock*, 1923, ink on paper, Zervos V no. 56.

83 Picasso, *Woman and Harlequin* (DC 133), 1915, watercolor and pencil on paper; $8\frac{5}{8} \times 5$ in. (21.1×12.5 cm.). Signed verso u.l. in pencil: Picasso/1915. Zervos II** no. 559; Douglas Cooper, *Picasso et le Théâtre* (Paris, Editions cercle d'art, 1967), no. 61; Kosinski no. 65.

84 The Picassos that Cooper purchased from Reber were *Still Life on a Table* (DC 67), 1923–24, oil on canvas, $51\frac{1}{2} \times 37\frac{1}{2}$ in. (129.5×95.3 cm.); Zervos IV no. 441; purchased October 1937 for £1,300; *Still Life on a Guéridon in front of a Window* (DC 103), 1919, gouache on paper, $11\frac{3}{4} \times 15\frac{1}{4}$ in. (29.8×38.7 cm.). Signed l.l.: Picasso 19. Stolen from the Château de Castille in 1974; *Guitar and Fruit Dish on Table* (DC 100), 1920, pastel on paper, $8\frac{1}{4} \times 10\frac{1}{2}$ in. (21×26.7 cm.). Signed u.r.: 26–11–20 Picasso. Zervos IV no. 214; and *Still Life with Mandolin on a Guéridon* (DC 99), 1921, watercolor, gouache, and graphite on wove paper, $10\frac{7}{8} \times 8\frac{3}{8}$ in. (27.6×21.2 cm.); Zervos IV no. 234; Kosinski no. 73.

85 There is evidence, for instance, of Reber's relationship with Valentin. In a letter of October 14, 1954, Reber wrote: "I knew Valentin already from his Berlin days before 1933, where I had been friendly with Flechtheim since before the first World War (Kannte ich Valentin noch aus seiner Berliner Zeit vor 1933, da ich mit Flechtheim seit vor dem ersten Weltkrieg befreundet war)." In a letter dated February 19, 1954, Reber inquired about a work by Picasso: "Picasso's so-called portrait of Gertrude Stein, which Nierendorf had taken with him (Picasso. sog. Portrait Gertrude Stein, was Nierendorf mitgenommen hatte)," as well as concerning the Beckmann portrait. See also letters dated November 4, 1953 and March 17, 1954; this correspondence is in the Curt Valentin archive in the library of the Museum of Modern Art, New York.

Concerning Reber's purchases of works by Gris at the Galerie Simon, see *Juan Gris: Letters, 1913–1927*, collected by Daniel-Henry Kahnweiler, trans. and ed. by Douglas Cooper (London: privately printed, 1956). The Valentin correspondence reveals, incidentally, that the publication of Gris's letters originally had been planned with Valentin.

86 My thanks to Walter Feilchenfeldt for providing me with documentation concerning some of these exhibitions: Berlin, Galerie Paul Cassirer, *Sammlung Reber*, 1913 and Darmstadt, Mathildenhöhe, *Gemälde Sammlung G.F. Reber, Barmen*, 1913.

87 The exhibition *Europäische Kunst der Gegenwart*, 1927, was sponsored by the Kunstverein. Another exhibition that included works from Reber's collection was *Die Kunst in unserer Zeit*, held March to May 1930 in Vienna, Kunstlerhaus, sponsored by the Gesellschaft zum Förderung Moderner Kunst.

88 See, for example, "Dr. Reber sees America," *Parnassus*, November 2, 1930, p. 23; and Edward Alden Jewell, "Dr. Reber on His Way," *The New York Times*, Sunday, November 2, 1930, section VIII, p. 14.

89 For Flechtheim's praise of Reber's collection, see the 1927 exhibition catalogue *Pablo Picasso* (Berlin, Galerie Alfred Flechtheim). Julius Meier-Graefe's remarks are recorded in his article "Die Sammlung Reber," *Frankfurter Zeitung*, May 22, 1931. Concerning Reber's collection of Picassos, Meier-Graefe wrote, "In Lausanne, besides innumerable drawings, he owns no fewer than seventy oil paintings (Er besizt in Lausanne ausser zahlosen Zeichnungen nicht weniger als siebzig Gemälde)."

90 An undated letter from Einstein to Cooper is preserved in the Cooper archive, Getty Center.

91 Concerning the galleries in this area, see Christopher Green, *Cubism and Its Enemies* (New Haven and London: Yale University Press, 1987) and Malcolm Gee, *Dealers, Critics and Collectors of Modern Painting: Aspects of the Parisian Art Market between 1910 and 1930* (New York: Garland, 1981).

92 For Pierre Loeb, see Paris, Musée Nationale d'Art Moderne, *L'Aventure de Pierre Loeb: La Galerie Pierre 1924–1964*, 1979; Madeleine Chapsal, "Entretien avec Pierre Loeb," *L'Express*, April 9, 1964; Pierre Loeb, *Voyages à travers la peinture* (Paris: Bordas, 1946); Pierre Loeb, *Regards sur la peinture* (Paris, 1950); J.J. Levêque, "Pierre Loeb," *Cimaise*, vol. 82 (October 1967); and Assouline, *L'Homme de l'art, D.-H. Kahnweiler* (Paris: Balland, 1988), pp. 273, 305, and 307.

93 The three Miró gouaches of 1935 purchased from Loeb in July 1936 were *Signs and Figurations* (DC 62), 1935, gouache on paper, 17½ × 13 in. (44.5 × 33 cm.); *Woman* (DC 61), 1935, gouache on paper, 14¾ × 12 in. (37 × 30 cm.); Perls Galleries nos. 6874/P4111; and *Planet, Moon, Woman, and Landscape* (DC 28), 1935, gouache on paper, 14½ × 12 in. (36.8 × 30.5 cm.); Perls Galleries nos. 6875/P4122.

94 Miró, *Figures* (DC 75), 1937, ink and wash on cardboard, 12 × 12 in. (30.5 × 30.5 cm.).

95 Léger, *Still Life on a Table* (DC 73), 1914, gouache and wash on paper, 25½ × 19½ in. (64.8 × 49.5 cm.); illus. Paris, Berggruen, *Léger, Contrastes de formes*, 1962. Léger, *Two Women Reclining* (DC card has no number), 1913, gouache on paper, 19½ × 25 in. (49.5 × 63.5 cm.). Gift to John Weyman in November 1937; present whereabouts unknown (see note 8, above). Léger, *Etude pour une nature morte* (DC 74), 1913, gouache on paper, 25½ × 19¾ in. (64.8 × 50.2 cm.); Basel, Galerie Beyeler, *Fernand Léger*, no. 6.

96 Braque, *Bottle and Glass — Standard* (DC 72), 1913, charcoal and pasted paper, 28¼ × 39¾ in. (72 × 101 cm.); Worms de Romilly and Jean Laude, *Braque: Le Cubisme: fin 1907–1914* (Paris: Maeght, 1982), no. 206.

97 Picasso, *The Guitar Player* (DC 37), 1912–13, pencil on paper, 25 × 19½ in. (63.5 × 49.5 cm.). Signed verso: Picasso. Zervos II** no. 394. Picasso, *Head of a Man* (DC 92), late 1908, ink and charcoal on paper, 24¼ × 18⅝ (61.6 × 47.4 cm.); Zervos II** no. 715; Kosinski no. 52.

98 Picasso, *Still Life with Garlands* (DC 98), 1918, oil and sand on canvas, 18³⁄₁₆ × 18⅛ in. (46.1 × 46 cm.); Zervos III no. 142.

99 The exhibition was at the Galerie Pierre June 12 to 27, 1925, accompanied by a catalogue by Benjamin Péret.

100 Mirós that Cooper purchased from Pierre Matisse: *Catalan Peasant Resting* (DC 27), 1936, oil on copper, 14⅜ × 10⅞ in. (36.5 × 27.5 cm.); Dupin, *Joan Miró*, no. 429; see Christie's London, *Impressionist and Modern Paintings and Sculpture*, March 28, 1988,

lot 39. *Two Women* (DC 22), 1935, oil on cardboard, 29½ × 41 in. (75 × 105 cm.); Dupin, *Joan Miró,* no. 412; *Personnage* or *The Lovers,* 1934, pastel on paper, 42 × 28 in. (108 × 72 cm.); Dupin, *Joan Miró,* no. 377; *Figure* (DC 24), 1934, pencil and gouache on paper, 39 × 28 in. (99.1 × 71.1 cm.); *Figure* (DC 30), 1935, gouache on paper, 12 × 14¾ in. (30.5 × 37.5 cm.); *Figure* (DC 63), 1935, gouache on paper, 11¾ × 14½ in. (29.8 × 36.8 cm.); *Bird, Shooting Star, and Landscape* (DC 31), 1935, gouache on paper, 14½ × 12 in. (36.8 × 30.5 cm.); *Figure at the Window* (DC 25), 1935, gouache on paper, 14½ × 11¾ in. (36.8 × 29.8 cm.); Perls Galleries nos. 13656/P9674; *Composition* (DC 79), 1937, gouache on black paper, 25 × 19½ in. (63.5 × 49.5 cm.); *Composition* (DC 76), 1937, gouache on black paper, 25½ × 19½ in. (64 × 50 cm.); and *Composition* (DC 80), 1937, gouache on paper, 18 × 24½ in. (45.7 × 62.2 cm.).

101 Other factors may have inspired Cooper's enthusiasm for Miró, for example Miró's inclusion in major exhibitions at the Museum of Modern Art in 1936 and 1937; the works presented in the *International Surrealist Exhibition* at the New Burlington Galleries in London in 1936, which included 22 paintings, drawings, and other objects dating from 1920 to 1934; and the interest in Spain as a result of the outbreak of the Civil War that year. The New York exhibitions were *Cubism and Abstract Art,* 1936 and *Fantastic Art, Dada, Surrealism* (catalogue by André Breton and Herbert Read), 1936–37.

102 On February 4, 1939, for $1,000 (£200), Cooper purchased Gris, *Violin with Guitar* (DC 3), 1913, oil on canvas, 31⅞ × 23⅝ in. (81 × 60 cm.); Cooper, *Gris* no. 40. On March 2, 1937, for £600, he purchased Picasso, *The Student* (DC 35), 1917–18, oil on canvas, 29 × 36½ in. (74 × 93 cm.); Zervos III no. 104.

103 From 1922 to 1923 the gallery was at 3, rue du Cherche-Midi; from 1925 to 1936 it was at 5, rue du Cherche-Midi; then 9ter, Boulevard de Montparnasse; and in 1938 it moved to 53, rue de Seine. In spring 1936 the gallery was renamed Bucher-Myrbor, reflecting a brief business association, lasting only until 1938, with Mme. Couturie, the wealthy wife of an Algerian senator — an alliance clearly necessitated by the impact of the financial crash.

104 Interview of September 8, 1989 with Mme. Bucher's nephew, Jean-François Jaeger, current owner of the Galerie Jeanne Bucher, conducted by the author's assistant, Lysa Hochroth; see also Assouline, *L'Homme de l'art, D.-H. Kahnweiler,* p. 305.

105 The three works by Gris purchased from Jeanne Bucher were *Still Life: Teapot and Glass* (DC 93), 1916, pencil on paper, 15⅜ × 11 in. (39.1 × 28 cm.); Kosinski no. 16; *Still Life: The Tobacco Pouch* (DC 94), 1918, pencil on paper, 12⅛ × 18¾ (31.8 × 47.6 cm.); Kosinski no. 19; and *Still Life: Apples, Glass and Knife* (DC 90), 1919, pencil on paper, 10¾ × 14 in. (27 × 35.5 cm.).

106 Lot 28, Léger, Study for *Curtain for La Création du monde* (DC 16), 1922, pencil on paper, 9⅞ × 7½ in. (25 × 19 cm.). At the same auction Cooper purchased Miró, *The Statue* (DC 26), 1925, oil on canvas, 25¾ × 32 in. (80 × 65 cm.); Dupin, *Joan Miró,* no. 123, lot 22. Other purchases at auction in 1937 were Miró, *Woman Chasing Bird* (no DC number), 1928, pencil and watercolor, lot 26(?) of the April sale of the Pertuisot collection at Christie's London; and, at the Hôtel Drouot, Paris, December 8, Picasso, *Head* (DC 83), 1910, charcoal on paper, 26½ × 18 in. (61.5 × 46 cm.); Zervos II** no. 395.

107 The three 1937 purchases from Bucher were Léger, *Man and Dog in a Landscape* (DC 15), 1921, pencil on paper, 10$\frac{3}{16}$ × 14⅞ in. (26.2 × 37.9 cm.); The Museum of Ulm. Léger, *Les Foreurs* (DC 56), 1916, ink and wash, 11¼ × 8 in. (28.6 × 20.3 cm.); Berlin, Staatliche Kunsthalle, *Fernand Léger,* 1980, p. 113, no. 20. Léger, *The Mason (Composition, le maçon,* DC 57), 1918, watercolor on paper, 13 × 9½ in. (33 × 24 cm.). See note 56, above, regarding the two 1937 purchases of Léger drawings from Léonce Rosenberg.

108 For subsequent purchases of Léger's war compositions, see Kosinski nos. 31, 32, and 48.

109 The members of the Peau de l'Ours group would pay 250 francs yearly toward the collective purchase of works of art. The collection was sold at the Hôtel Drouot on March 2, 1914, with each member refunded his original investment plus 3.5% interest. The main objective was to support young artists, who each received 20% from the proceeds of the sale. Level was reimbursed for his role as administrator, receiving an additional 20% payment. See André Level, *Souvenirs d'un collectionneur* (Paris: Alain Mazo, 1959), p. 17 and Guy Habasque, "Quand on vendait la peau de l'ours," *l'Oeil,* March 15, 1956.

110 See Assouline, *L'Homme de l'art, D.-H. Kahnweiler,* p. 241.

111 Level's support of the Cubists has been analyzed by Christopher Green and Malcolm Gee as an indication of the upmarket or snobbish connotations associated with Cubism in the twenties, one of the factors that kept the prices for these artists low. See Christopher Green, *Cubism and Its Enemies,* 1987, p. 137; also Malcolm Gee, *Dealers, Critics, and Collectors of Modern Painting,* 1977, pp. 160 and 175–83.

112 Gris, *Houses on the Place Ravignan,* Paris (DC 95), 1911, oil on canvas, 20½ × 13⅜ in. (52 × 34 cm.); Cooper, *Gris* no. 9, purchased February 1938 for £50. Two of Cooper's purchases from the Galerie Percier, both Picassos, have been discussed above; see p. 14 and note 50.

113 Zak was a member of *les Formistes* from 1917 to 1921, and participated in the exhibition *Club des artistes Polonais* in November 1917.

114 Gris, *Mandolin and Glass on a Table* (DC 7), 1913, watercolor and charcoal on paper, 25 × 18 in. (46.8 × 63 cm.). See Baden-Baden, Staatliche Kunsthalle, *Juan Gris*, 1974, Zeichnung 14.

115 Gris, *Portrait of the Artist's Mother* (DC 97), c. March 1912, oil on canvas, 21 13/16 × 18 1/4 in. (55.4 × 46.3 cm.). It was exhibited in Berlin, Galerie Flechtheim, *In Memoriam Juan Gris*, 1930, no. 3. Later Cooper included it in The Los Angeles County Museum of Art and New York, The Metropolitan Museum of Art, *The Cubist Epoch*, 1970–71, no. 109, illus. pl. 221; Cooper, *Essential Cubism* no. 59; Cooper, *Gris* no. 14.

116 Interview by the author's assistant, Lysa Hochroth, with Jean-Pierre Bénézit (Galerie Bénézit, Paris), treasurer of the Comité Professionel des Galeries de l'Art, on September 20, 1989 provided much of this background information. According to Bénézit and his father Henri, Maratier and his colleague Madame Berger later worked at the Galerie d'Institut on the rue de Seine.

117 The undated letter from Maratier to Cooper is preserved in the Cooper records in the Douglas Cooper Collection (the original handwritten letter contains no accents). Maratier wrote:

> *My dear friend,*
> *Alas, with all these events, just as the sale of the Gris was about to be finalized, my client preferred to wait and not to give a firm response until the bad days seemed at an end. I remain in touch with Dr. Reber or rather with Mlle. Fritsch. Do you know a J. Gris, probably an early work that is owned by a Miss Netter, rue Pernety? It's a naturalistic oil representing two masks, a background of blue and pink drapery — format 12. It must be a canvas executed between the Assiette au Beurre period and the beginning of the Cubist period. The Kunsthalle Berne is organizing an exhibition of Braque-Gris-Picasso for the month of May. They asked me for your picture. I mentioned it to Mlle. Fritsch who should mention it to Dr. Reber who should fix it up for me.... A real administration and quite amusing. Business is at a complete standstill and everybody is complaining, but if everything goes back to normal I hope to have a very good season. And after all, it's no use being pessimistic. Most sincerely, Maratier*
>
> *(Mon cher ami,*
> *Hélas avec tous ces événements au moment où la vente du Gris allait enfin se terminer, mon client a préféré attendre et ne donnera une réponse ferme que si les mauvais jours semblent terminés. Je reste en rapport avec le Docteur Reber ou plutôt avec Mademoiselle Fritsch. Connais-tu un J. Gris probablement de jeunesse qui se trouve chez une demoiselle Netter, rue Pernety. C'est une peinture à l'huile naturaliste représentant 2 masques une fond fait d'une draperie bleue et rose — format environ 12. Ce doit etre une toile exécutée entre l'époque de l'Assiette au beurre et le début de la période cubiste. Le Kunsthalle de Berne organise pour le mois de mai une exposition Braque-Gris-Picasso. On m'a demandé ton tableau. J'en ai parlé à Mademoiselle Fritsch qui doit en référer au Dr. Reber qui doit me fixer.... Une véritable administration assez amusante. Les affaires sont complètement arrêtées et tout le monde se plainait mais si tout rentre dans l'ordre j'ai espoir d'avoir une très bonne saison. Et après tout il ne sert à rien d'être pessimiste. Très sincèrement Maratier).*

This letter refers to the exhibition *Picasso, Braque, Gris, Léger, Bores, Beaudin, Vines* at Bern Kunsthalle, May 6 to June 14, 1939.

118 The exhibitions included *Alberto Giacometti* (1932 — this was the artist's first one-person exhibition in Paris); *Le Surréalisme en 1933* (January 14 to February 5, 1933); *Max Jacob* (January 19 to February 1, 1933); *Surréalisme* (June 7 to 20, 1933); and *Dali* (June 20 to 30, 1933).

119 Among their notable exhibitions were *Compositions par André Derain* (May 10 to 31, 1935), *Aquarelles et baignades de Paul Cézanne* (June 3 to 17, 1935), *Exposition Georges Braque* (June 19 to July 4, 1935), *Dessins de Henri Matisse* (November 1935), *Dessins de Picasso* (February 14 to March 11, 1936), *Dali* (July 6 to 30, 1937), *Wolfgang Paalen* (June 21 to July 5, 1938), and *Léger peintures* (November 22 to December 6, 1938).

120 Colle died in Mexico in 1949. After the war Renou set up partnership with Monsieur Poyet, a dealer from Lyon, who had recently established himself on rue de la Boëtie. The Galerie Renou & Poyet flourished after the war; the owners maintained broad international contacts with colleagues in London, for instance, with galleries that included the Mayor Gallery and Reid & Lefèvre. Renou retired about 1965 and died in 1973. The gallery is currently directed by M. Maurice Covo, who graciously provided a great deal of this background information in interviews with the author's assistant, Lysa Hochroth, on September 13 and 21, 1989.

121 Valentine Dudensing and Albert Skira were particularly important clients of the gallery Renou & Colle; the former purchased a number of Picassos in 1936. Gallery records from 1936 indicate the following clients: Georges Salle, Peter Watson, Raoul La Roche, Paul Rosenberg, and Albert Sarrault. Edward James, the noted collector of Surrealism, purchased two Picasso drawings on February 26, 1936 and an oil by de Chirico. In 1937 James was among a number of buyers of works by Dali; another buyer was the Leicester Gallery in London. Alfred Barr apparently purchased Balthus' *Portrait of André Derain* from Renou & Colle. Not surprisingly, the gallery maintained close relationships with the other Paris dealers. In 1956 Renou & Colle purchased Picasso's *Parade* with Pierre Loeb at auction. Records indicate that Loeb purchased a Picasso drawing on January 11, 1937. Livengood and Maratier from the Galerie de Beaune also bought from Renou & Colle. On November 7, 1939, a Picasso portrait was purchased from G.F. Reber; the work was sold June 19, 1940 to Dundensing.

122 Gallery records indicate only that Cooper bought two draw-

ings for Fr. 3,000. These were from a group of 12 drawings that the gallery had purchased directly from the artist on February 29 and March 20, 1936. Perhaps the gallery never recorded the third drawing, or the records are incomplete. The three Picasso drawings in Cooper's records are *Standing Woman* (DC 43), 1911–12, ink and wash on paper, $21\frac{11}{16} \times 8\frac{9}{16}$ in. (55.2 × 21.7 cm.); Kosinski no. 56; purchased February 1936; *The Card Player* (DC 38), 1914, pencil on paper, $12\frac{3}{8} \times 9\frac{3}{16}$ in. (31.5 × 23.3 cm.); Kosinski no. 63; purchased June 1937; and *Still Life with Table and Dish of Pears* (DC 88), 1912, charcoal with graphite on Ingres paper; $24\frac{3}{8} \times 18\frac{5}{8}$ in. (62 × 47.3 cm.); Kosinski no. 58; purchased 1937.

123 The four works by Picasso acquired in 1939 from G.F. Reber were *Bacchus* (DC 140), 1906, ink drawing, $7\frac{1}{2} \times 6$ in. (19.1 x 15.2 cm.), a gift; *Standing Female Nude* (DC 141), see note 76, above; *Bottle of "Bass" and Guitar* (no DC number), see note 80, above; and *Man and Woman* (DC 183), 1921, charcoal and pastel on board, $40\frac{1}{2} \times 28$ in. (103 × 71 cm.); Zervos IV no. 224. The Gris was *Still Life with Guitar on a Table* (DC 126), see note 75, above.

124 The Gris from Willi Raeber was *Harlequin's Head* (DC 130), 1924, oil on canvas, $13\frac{3}{4} \times 9\frac{1}{2}$ in. (35 × 24 cm.); Cooper, *Gris* no. 476. Exhibited: Berlin, Galerie Flechtheim, *In Memoriam Juan Gris*, 1930, no. 38.

The two works by Gris purchased from Ronald Fleming were *The Book* (DC 124), 1924, oil on canvas, $9\frac{1}{2} \times 13$ in. (24 × 33 cm.); Cooper, *Gris* no. 483; and *Still Life with Bottle and Cigars* (DC 123), 1912, charcoal, colored pencil or oil crayon, gouache, and ink with pasted paper on gray paper, $18\frac{11}{16} \times 12\frac{1}{4}$ in. (47.5 × 31 cm.); Kosinski no. 14.

125 A few galleries, including Galerie Jeanne Bucher, did remain open during the occupation. Galerie Bucher apparently became a center for the Resistance, and it defiantly presented a one-person show of Kandinsky in 1936. Galerie Zak also continued to house exhibitions during the war.

126 See John Richardson, "Remembering Douglas Cooper," *The New York Review of Books*, April 25, 1985, p. 24.

127 The two works were Braque, *Still Life: Fruit Dish and Newspaper* (DC 118), 1919, ink and pencil on paper, $7\frac{11}{16} \times 10\frac{5}{8}$ in. (19.5 × 27 cm.); Kosinski no. 7; and Picasso, *Nude* (DC 142), 1906, ink and wash on paper, 25 × 18 in. (63.5 × 45.7 cm.); formerly collection Alfred Flechtheim, Berlin.

128 A decade later, between 1955 and 1958, Cooper sold 15 of the Klees, all except one to Heinz Berggruen. This concentrated sale of almost all of the Klees that he owned was probably necessitated by the costs of the newly refurbished Château de Castille, into which Cooper moved in 1951. Heinz Berggruen asserts that the sale was prompted by Cooper's disenchantment with the Klees, a lack of interest in the works, and a desire to concentrate more exclusively on the major thrust of his collection, namely Cubism (author's conversation with Heinz Berggruen, December 3, 1989).

129 Léger, *View of Paris* (DC 122), 1912, oil on canvas, 18 × 15 in. (45 × 27.5 cm.); illus. Cooper, *Léger* p. 43.

130 Amedeo Modigliani, *Nude* (DC 148), c. 1919, watercolor and pencil on paper, $16\frac{3}{4} \times 10$ in. (42.5 × 25.4 cm.).

131 Interestingly, the collector Dr. Reber, so important to Cooper's collecting, also figured in a minor way in the Allied Report, for he worked briefly for Walter Andreas Hofer, the art advisor to Reichsmarschall Hermann Goering, and helped to establish contacts for Goering with dealers and collectors in Switzerland and Italy.

132 The works Cooper purchased from Erna Reber were for £15, Léger, Study for *Still Life with Bust* (DC 120), 1924, pencil, colored pencil, and watercolor on paper, $12\frac{15}{16} \times 9\frac{15}{16}$ in. (31.4 × 25.2 cm.); Kosinski no. 41; for £15, Léger, *Composition with Musical Instruments* (DC 121), 1925, crayon on paper, $11\frac{1}{2} \times 8\frac{1}{2}$ in. (29.2 × 21.6 cm.); and for £100, Gris, *Landscape at Beaulieu* (DC 129), 1916, oil on panel, $21\frac{5}{8} \times 15$ in. (55 × 38 cm.); Cooper, *Gris* no. 201.

133 For example, Braque's *Big Trees at l'Estaque* (DC 119), 1908, oil on canvas, $31\frac{5}{8} \times 23\frac{11}{16}$ in. (80.4 × 60.2 cm.); Cooper, *Essential Cubism* no. 4; purchased in 1945 for £300 from Paul Adamidi Frasheri Bey in Geneva, had once also been part of Reber's collection. Bey, a friend or associate of Reber, a frequent visitor at Reber's Château de Béthusy, and, like Reber, an enthusiast of the occult, purchased this Braque in 1934. Note also that Cooper purchased a small watercolor by Léger, *The Sappers* (DC 205), from Bey in 1945. See Kosinski no. 31. Similarly, the Gris *Fruit Dish* (DC 125), 1918, oil on panel, $24\frac{3}{8} \times 15\frac{3}{8}$ in. (62 × 39 cm.); Cooper *Gris* no. 251; purchased from Luis Neumann in Basel in 1945 for £170, had at one time been part of Reber's collection. Reber had also owned Gris, *Fruit Dish and Bottle of Beaune* (DC 107), 1917; Cooper, *Gris* no. 236; which Cooper purchased from Neumann, Zurich, in November 1938 for £100. See also note 17, above, regarding Picasso's *Seated Woman Holding a Book*. Although purchased by Cooper in 1936 from Zwemmer in London, it was formerly in the Reber collection.

134 In 1946, besides the works by Paul Klee mentioned above and two lithographs by André Masson purchased from the Galerie Simon, Cooper bought few works. These included a 1907 Picasso ink drawing from the Redfern Gallery and etchings by Matisse and Picasso from the Leicester Gallery. From 1948 to 1950 he purchased only a few prints, these from the Galerie Louise Leiris.

135 My thanks to Gavin Bingham from the Bank for International Settlements, Basel, for his assistance in providing the necessary statistical information for this brief analysis. Because of incomplete documentation, it is not possible to provide an absolutely certain list of Cooper's acquisitions at this time. For example, with two works by Léger, we are uncertain of either date of purchase (in the case of *Composition with Two Dancers,* 1929, oil, $35 \times 51\frac{1}{8}$ in. [89×130 cm.]; Basel, Galerie Beyeler, *Léger,* 1981, no. 24); or where the work was acquired from (as with *Two Figures* [DC 104], 1920, ink and wash on paper, $14\frac{15}{16} \times 12\frac{5}{16}$ in. [38×31.2 cm.]; Kosinski no. 35; purchased October 1938 for £5).

136 See the partial bibliography of Cooper's art history and criticism, compiled by Caroline Brooke, included in Kosinski.

CHECKLIST OF THE EXHIBITION

1.
Georges Braque
Standing Nude, 1907
Ink on paper, $12\frac{3}{16} \times 7\frac{7}{8}$ in. (30.9 × 20 cm.)
The Douglas Cooper Collection, Churchglade Ltd.

2.
Georges Braque
Standing Nude, 1907
Etching, $19\frac{1}{4} \times 12\frac{3}{4}$ in. (48.9 × 32.4 cm.)
The Douglas Cooper Collection, Churchglade Ltd.

3.
Georges Braque
Still Life with Bottle of Gin on a Table (Fox), 1911
Etching with drypoint on Arches paper, $25\frac{3}{4} \times 19\frac{13}{16}$ in. (65.3 × 50.3 cm.)
The Douglas Cooper Collection, Churchglade Ltd.

4.
Georges Braque
Still Life with Dice, summer 1912
Charcoal on paper, $9\frac{13}{16} \times 12\frac{13}{16}$ in. (25 × 32.5 cm.)
Private collection

5.
Georges Braque
Fruit Dish and Glass, September 1912
Charcoal and printed paper pasted on paper, $24\frac{3}{4} \times 18$ in. (62.8 × 45.7 cm.)
Private collection

6.
Georges Braque
Still Life with Guitar on a Table, 1917
Ink on paper with pencil, $7\frac{1}{2} \times 10\frac{15}{16}$ in. (19.1 × 27.8 cm.)
The Douglas Cooper Collection, Churchglade Ltd.

7.
Georges Braque
Still Life: Fruit Dish and Newspaper, 1919
Ink and pencil on paper, $7\frac{11}{16} \times 10\frac{5}{8}$ in. (19.5 × 27 cm.)
The Douglas Cooper Collection, Churchglade Ltd.

8.
Georges Braque
Studio VIII, 1952–55
Oil on canvas, $52 \times 77\frac{1}{2}$ in. (132.1 × 196.9 cm.)
Private collection

9.
Georges Braque
Fire Bird, c. 1954
Oil and charcoal on paper pasted to panel, $10\frac{15}{16} \times 19\frac{1}{4}$ in. (27.7 × 48.9 cm.)
Collection John Richardson

10.
Georges Braque
Maquette for Catalogue, Tate Gallery Exhibition, 1956
Gouache, pasted paper, and ink on paper pasted to cardboard, $9\frac{1}{2} \times 7\frac{3}{8}$ in. (24.2 × 18.8 cm.)
The Douglas Cooper Collection, Churchglade Ltd.

11.
Juan Gris
Still Life with Pitcher, 1910
Charcoal with white chalk or gouache on paper, $18\frac{15}{16} \times 12\frac{5}{8}$ in. (48 × 31.3 cm.)
The Douglas Cooper Collection, Churchglade Ltd.

12.
Still Life with Oil Lamp, 1911
Charcoal on paper, $18\frac{7}{8} \times 12\frac{3}{8}$ in. (47.9 × 31.5 cm.)
The Douglas Cooper Collection, Churchglade Ltd.

13.
Juan Gris
Still Life: Soup Tureen and Glass, 1911
Pencil on paper, $10\frac{9}{16} \times 7\frac{7}{8}$ in. (26.8 × 20 cm.)
The Douglas Cooper Collection, Churchglade Ltd.

14.
Juan Gris
Still Life with Cup and Glass, 1911
Pencil on paper, $14\frac{1}{16} \times 12\frac{5}{8}$ in. (35.7 × 32 cm.)
The Douglas Cooper Collection, Churchglade Ltd.

15.
Juan Gris
Houses on the Place Ravignan, Paris, 1911
Oil on canvas, $20\frac{1}{2} \times 13\frac{3}{8}$ in. (52 × 34 cm.)
Private collection

16.
Juan Gris
Portrait of the Artist's Mother, c. March 1912
Oil on canvas, $21\frac{13}{16} \times 18\frac{1}{4}$ in. (55.4 × 46.3 cm.)
Private collection

17.
Juan Gris
Still Life with Bottle and Cigars, 1912
Charcoal, colored pencil or oil crayon, gouache, and ink with pasted paper on gray paper, $18\frac{11}{16} \times 12\frac{1}{4}$ in. (47.5 × 31 cm.)
The Douglas Cooper Collection, Churchglade Ltd.

18.
Juan Gris
Guitar, verso: *Violin*, 1913
Pencil on paper, $25\frac{9}{16} \times 9\frac{11}{16}$ in. (65 × 50 cm.)
Collection Jasper Johns

19.
Juan Gris
Still Life: Teapot and Glass, 1916
Pencil on paper, $15\frac{3}{8} \times 11$ in. (39.1 × 28 cm.)
The Douglas Cooper Collection, Churchglade Ltd.

20.
Juan Gris
Copy after Cézanne's *Portrait of Louis Guillaume*, 1916
Pencil on paper, $13\frac{15}{16} \times 10\frac{11}{16}$ in. (35.5 × 27.2 cm.)
The Douglas Cooper Collection, Churchglade Ltd.

21.
Juan Gris
Copy after Cézanne's *Portrait of Mme. Cézanne*, 1916
Pencil on paper, $8\frac{3}{4} \times 8\frac{9}{16}$ in. (22.3 × 21.7 cm.)
The Douglas Cooper Collection, Churchglade Ltd.

22.
Juan Gris
Still Life with Guitar on a Table, 1916
Oil on canvas, $36\frac{3}{16} \times 23\frac{3}{8}$ in.
(92 × 59.3 cm.)
Private collection

23.
Juan Gris
Still Life: The Tobacco Pouch, 1918
Pencil on paper, $12\frac{1}{8} \times 18\frac{3}{4}$ in.
(31.8 × 47.6 cm.)
Private collection

24.
Juan Gris
Drawing for *Seated Harlequin with Guitar,* 1919
Pencil on paper, $13\frac{1}{4} \times 9\frac{15}{16}$ in.
(33.8 × 25.2 cm.)
Galerie Louise Leiris, Paris

25.
Fernand Léger
Standing Nude, 1911
Ink on paper, $12\frac{7}{8} \times 9\frac{5}{16}$ in.
(32.6 × 23.7 cm.)
The Douglas Cooper Collection, Churchglade Ltd.

26.
Fernand Léger
Study for an *Abundance,* 1912
Ink on paper, $12\frac{1}{8} \times 7\frac{9}{16}$ in.
(30.8 × 19.2 cm.)
The Douglas Cooper Collection, Churchglade Ltd.

27.
Fernand Léger
Two Reclining Women, 1913
Gouache and wash on paper,
$19\frac{3}{4} \times 25\frac{5}{8}$ in. (50.2 × 65.1 cm.)
The Metropolitan Museum of Art, New York; gift of Mr. and Mrs. William R. Acquavella, 1986

28.
Fernand Léger
Still Life, 1913
Gouache and oil on paper, $18\frac{5}{8} \times 23\frac{3}{8}$ in.
(47.7 × 59.3 cm.)
Private collection

29.
Fernand Léger
Still Life on a Table, 1914
Gouache and wash on paper,
$25\frac{1}{2} \times 19\frac{1}{2}$ in. (64.8 × 49.5 cm.)
The Metropolitan Museum of Art, New York; gift of Mr. and Mrs. William R. Acquavella, 1986.

30.
Fernand Léger
The Sappers, 1916
Watercolor and ink on paper, $9 \times 5\frac{3}{4}$ in.
(23 × 14.5 cm.)
The Douglas Cooper Collection, Churchglade Ltd.

31.
Fernand Léger
Two Dead, 1916
Brown ink and pencil on paper postcard,
$4\frac{13}{16} \times 3\frac{1}{2}$ in. (12.3 × 8.9 cm.)
The Douglas Cooper Collection, Churchglade Ltd.

32.
Fernand Léger
Drawing for *The Cardplayers,* 1916–17
Wash and pencil on paper, $20\frac{3}{4} \times 14\frac{7}{8}$ in.
(52.7 × 37.8 cm.)
Private collection

33.
Fernand Léger
Man in a Mechanical Landscape, 1918
Ink and wash with pencil, watercolor, and gouache on paper, $9\frac{5}{8} \times 12\frac{7}{8}$ in.
(24.5 × 32.7 cm.)
Private collection

34.
Fernand Léger
Two Figures, 1920
Ink and wash on paper, $14\frac{15}{16} \times 12\frac{5}{16}$ in.
(38 × 31.2 cm.)
Private collection

35.
Fernand Léger
Three Women, 1921
Pencil on paper, $12\frac{3}{8} \times 16\frac{7}{16}$ in.
(31.4 × 41.8 cm.)
The Douglas Cooper Collection, Churchglade Ltd.

36.
Fernand Léger
Man and Dog in a Landscape, 1921
Pencil on paper, $10\frac{5}{16} \times 14\frac{7}{8}$ in.
(26.2 × 37.9 cm.)
The Museum of Ulm, Permanent Loan from the State of Baden-Württemberg

37.
Fernand Léger
Study for *Curtain for La Création du monde,* 1922
Pencil on paper, $9\frac{7}{8} \times 7\frac{1}{2}$ in. (25 × 19 cm.)
Jean-Claude Bellier

38.
Fernand Léger
Still Life with Bust, 1924
Oil on canvas, $25\frac{1}{2} \times 19\frac{5}{8}$ in.
(64.6 × 49.7 cm.)
Private collection

39.
Fernand Léger
Two Men in a Stairway, 1924
Pencil on paper, $11\frac{11}{16} \times 10\frac{1}{16}$ in.
(29.3 × 25.5 cm.)
The Douglas Cooper Collection, Churchglade Ltd.

40.
Fernand Léger
Still Life with Coffee Pot, 1924
Pencil on paper, $12\frac{1}{2} \times 9\frac{7}{16}$ in.
(31.8 × 23.9 cm.)
The Douglas Cooper Collection, Churchglade Ltd.

41.
Fernand Léger
The Siphon, 1924
Graphite and colored pencil with watercolor on paper, $10\frac{11}{16} \times 7\frac{7}{16}$ in.
(27.1 × 19 cm.)
The Douglas Cooper Collection, Churchglade Ltd.

42.
Fernand Léger
Study for *Still Life with Bust,* 1924
Pencil, colored pencil, and watercolor on paper, $12\frac{15}{16} \times 9\frac{15}{16}$ in. (31.4 × 25.2 cm.)
The Douglas Cooper Collection, Churchglade Ltd.

43.
Fernand Léger
Composition with Checker Game, 1926
Gouache on paper, $19\frac{1}{8} \times 16\frac{11}{16}$ in.
(48.6×42.4 cm.)
The Douglas Cooper Collection,
Churchglade Ltd.

44.
Fernand Léger
Gloves, 1933
Black ink on paper, $12\frac{3}{4} \times 9\frac{7}{8}$ in.
(32.4×25.1 cm.)
The Douglas Cooper Collection,
Churchglade Ltd.

45.
Fernand Léger
Composition, 1936
Oil on canvas, $14\frac{1}{2} \times 17\frac{5}{8}$ in.
(36.8×44.8 cm.)
The Fogg Museum of Art, Harvard
University, Cambridge, Massachusetts;
gift of Mr. and Mrs. Harold Gershinowitz

46.
Fernand Léger
Woman with Hand before her Face, Sketch for
Composition with Two Parrots, 1939
Pen and ink on paper, $15\frac{3}{8} \times 12\frac{5}{8}$ in.
(39.4×32.1 cm.)
Private collection

47.
Fernand Léger
Maquette for Catalogue, Tate Gallery
Exhibition, 1950
Gouache and pencil on paper,
$12\frac{5}{8} \times 9\frac{7}{16}$ in. (32×24 cm.)
The Douglas Cooper Collection,
Churchglade Ltd.

48.
Fernand Léger
Maquette for Catalogue, Tate Gallery
Exhibition, 1950
Gouache and pencil on paper,
$12\frac{5}{8} \times 9\frac{7}{16}$ in. (32×24 cm.)
The Douglas Cooper Collection,
Churchglade Ltd.

49.
Fernand Léger
Construction Worker, Legs, 1951
Ink and wash, $25 \times 19\frac{1}{8}$ in.
(63.5×48.5 cm.)
The Douglas Cooper Collection,
Churchglade Ltd.

50.
Fernand Léger
Maquette for Catalogue for *Dessins de
Guerre*, 1956
Gouache on folded paper, $12 \times 7\frac{5}{8}$ in.
(30.6×18.5 cm.)
The Douglas Cooper Collection,
Churchglade Ltd.

51.
Pablo Picasso
The Soldier, c. 1901
Crayon on paper, $6 \times 4\frac{1}{4}$ in.
(15.2×10.8 cm.)
Private collection

52.
Pablo Picasso
Standing Female Nude, 1906–07
Black ink and red gouache with wash on
paper, $24\frac{1}{4} \times 16\frac{11}{16}$ in. (61.5×42.4 cm.)
Private collection

53.
Pablo Picasso
Study for *Les Demoiselles d'Avignon*, verso:
Amazone, spring 1907
Charcoal on paper, $18\frac{3}{4} \times 25\frac{1}{8}$ in.
(47.6×63.7 cm.)
Kunstmuseum Basel, Print Department; gift
of Douglas Cooper

54.
Pablo Picasso
Three Figures under a Tree, winter 1907–08
Oil on canvas, 39×39 in. (99×99 cm.)
Musée Picasso, Paris

55.
Pablo Picasso
Head of a Man, late 1908
Ink and charcoal on paper, $24\frac{1}{4} \times 18\frac{5}{8}$ in.
(61.6×47.4 cm.)
Private collection

56.
Pablo Picasso
Still Life with Chocolate Pot, early 1909
Watercolor on paper, $24\frac{5}{16} \times 18\frac{11}{16}$ in.
(61.7×47.5 cm.)
Private collection

57.
Pablo Picasso
Head of a Woman, Casket, and Apple, 1909
Pencil on paper, $9 \times 12\frac{7}{8}$ in.
(22.9×31.6 cm.)
The Douglas Cooper Collection,
Churchglade Ltd.

58.
Pablo Picasso
Still Life: Sugar Bowl and Fan, 1909–10
Watercolor on Ingres paper, $12\frac{7}{16} \times 16\frac{7}{8}$ in.
(31.5×43 cm.)
The Douglas Cooper Collection,
Churchglade Ltd.

59.
Pablo Picasso
Standing Woman, 1911–12
Ink and wash on paper, $21\frac{11}{16} \times 8\frac{9}{16}$ in.
(55.2×21.7 cm.)
Private collection

60.
Pablo Picasso
The Clarinet Player, 1911–12
Oil on canvas, $42\frac{15}{16} \times 27\frac{1}{8}$ in.
(106×69 cm.)
Thyssen-Bornemisza Collection, Lugano,
Switzerland

61.
Pablo Picasso
Composition with a Violin, 1912
Pencil, charcoal, gouache, and pasted
newspaper on paper, $24\frac{1}{16} \times 18\frac{1}{4}$ in.
(61.1×46.5 cm.)
Private collection

62.
Pablo Picasso
Still Life with Bottle of Marc, 1912
Drypoint etching, $28\frac{7}{16} \times 21\frac{5}{8}$ in.
(72.2×54.9 cm.)
The Douglas Cooper Collection,
Churchglade Ltd.

63.
Pablo Picasso
Still Life with Table and Dish of Pears, 1912
Charcoal with graphite on Ingres paper, $24\frac{3}{8} \times 18\frac{5}{8}$ in. (62×47.3 cm.)
The Douglas Cooper Collection, Churchglade Ltd.

64.
Pablo Picasso
Still Life with Dead Birds, summer 1912
Oil on canvas, $18\frac{1}{8} \times 25\frac{5}{8}$ in. (46×65 cm.)
Museo del Prado, Madrid

65.
Pablo Picasso
Bottle of "Bass" and Guitar, 1912–13
Pastel, charcoal, and stenciled black ink on Ingres paper, $18\frac{3}{4} \times 25$ in. (47.7×63.5 cm.)
The Douglas Cooper Collection, Churchglade Ltd.

66.
Pablo Picasso
Still Life: Glass and Bottle of "Bass," 1914
Pencil, gouache, and pasted paper on paper mounted on cardboard, $9\frac{9}{16} \times 7\frac{9}{16}$ in. (24.3×19.2 cm.)
The Douglas Cooper Collection, Churchglade Ltd.

67.
Pablo Picasso
The Card Player, 1914
Pencil on paper, $12\frac{3}{8} \times 9\frac{3}{16}$ in. (31.5×23.3 cm.)
Private collection

68.
Pablo Picasso
Bearded Man Playing a Guitar, 1914
Pencil highlighted with watercolor and gouache, $19\frac{1}{2} \times 15$ in. (48.9×37.2 cm.)
Private collection

69.
Pablo Picasso
Woman and Harlequin, 1915
Watercolor and pencil on paper, $8\frac{5}{8} \times 5$ in. (21.1×12.5 cm.)
The Douglas Cooper Collection, Churchglade Ltd.

70.
Pablo Picasso
Je t'aime Gaby, 1916
Five oval watercolors and two oval photographs, each: $1\frac{5}{8} \times 1\frac{3}{8}$ in. (4.2×3.5 cm); rectangular sheet with text and decorative border: $2\frac{9}{16} \times 6\frac{7}{8}$ in. (6.5×17.5 cm.); rectangular sheet of text: $1\frac{1}{8} \times 5\frac{3}{16}$ in. (3×13.2 cm.)
Collection William McCarty-Cooper

71.
Pablo Picasso
Three Letters with Provençal Interiors, 1916
Watercolor and ink on paper
Three rectangular pages: a) bedroom interior, $6\frac{7}{8} \times 5\frac{1}{8}$ in. (17.5×13 cm.); b) kitchen interior, $6\frac{7}{8} \times 6$ in. (17.5×15.3 cm.); c) dining room interior, $6\frac{7}{8} \times 4\frac{3}{8}$ in. (17.5×11 cm.)
Collection William McCarty-Cooper

72.
Pablo Picasso
Ton amour est pour moi ma vie, 1916
Watercolor on paper, $24\frac{11}{16} \times 2\frac{1}{4}$ in. (62.8×5.8 cm.); with souvenirs of Gaby Lespinasse: wooden bead necklace, three photographs, an additional small drawing, and the *livret de famille* of Gaby Lespinasse
Collection William McCarty-Cooper

73.
Pablo Picasso
Still Life with Garlands, 1918
Oil and sand on canvas, $18\frac{3}{16} \times 18\frac{1}{8}$ in. (46.1×46 cm.)
Private collection

74.
Pablo Picasso
Pierrot, 1918
Pencil on paper, $10\frac{3}{4} \times 7\frac{5}{8}$ in. (27.3×19.4 cm.)
The Douglas Cooper Collection, Churchglade Ltd.

75.
Pablo Picasso
Pierrot and Harlequin, 1920
Gouache on paper, $8\frac{1}{4} \times 10\frac{7}{16}$ in. (21×26.5 cm.)
The Douglas Cooper Collection, Churchglade Ltd.

76.
Pablo Picasso
Standing Female Nude with Drapery, 1920
Ink on paper, $9\frac{1}{2} \times 6\frac{3}{16}$ in. (24.1×15.7 cm.)
The Douglas Cooper Collection, Churchglade Ltd.

77.
Pablo Picasso
Still Life with Mandolin on a Guéridon, 1921
Watercolor, gouache, and graphite on wove paper, $10\frac{7}{8} \times 8\frac{3}{8}$ in. (27.6×21.2 cm.)
The Douglas Cooper Collection, Churchglade Ltd.

78.
Pablo Picasso
Still Life with Fruit Dish and Mandolin, 1932
Oil on canvas, $38\frac{1}{4} \times 51\frac{3}{16}$ in. (96.8×129.9 cm.)
Private collection

79.
Pablo Picasso
Boy with a Popsicle, 1938
Charcoal on paper, $26\frac{9}{16} \times 17\frac{1}{2}$ in. (67.5×44.5 cm.)
The Douglas Cooper Collection, Churchglade Ltd.

80.
Pablo Picasso
Reclining Female Nude, 1961
Pencil with white oil crayon on heavy notebook paper, $9\frac{1}{2} \times 12\frac{9}{16}$ in. (24×32 cm.)
The Douglas Cooper Collection, Churchglade Ltd.

81.
Pablo Picasso
Study for *Déjeuner sur l'herbe,* 1962
Pencil on notebook paper, $10\frac{5}{8} \times 16\frac{3}{4}$ in. (27×42.5 cm.)
The Douglas Cooper Collection, Churchglade Ltd.

82.
Pablo Picasso
Study for *Déjeuner sur l'herbe,* 1962
Pencil on notebook paper, $10\frac{3}{4} \times 13\frac{13}{16}$ in. (27.3×35 cm.)
The Douglas Cooper Collection, Churchglade Ltd.

83.
Pablo Picasso
Study for *Déjeuner sur l'herbe,* 1962
Oil pencil and colored pencils on notebook paper, $9\frac{7}{16} \times 12\frac{5}{8}$ in. (24 × 32 cm.)
The Douglas Cooper Collection, Churchglade Ltd.

84.
Pablo Picasso
Achilles, 1962
Pencil on notebook paper, $10\frac{13}{16} \times 8\frac{3}{8}$ in. (27.5 × 21.3 cm.)
The Douglas Cooper Collection, Churchglade Ltd.

85.
Pablo Picasso
Cavalier, 1962
Pencil on notebook paper, $8\frac{3}{8} \times 10\frac{13}{16}$ in. (21.3 × 27.5 cm.)
The Douglas Cooper Collection, Churchglade Ltd.

86.
David Hockney
Portrait of Douglas Cooper, 1974
Colored pencil on paper, 17 × 14 in. (43.3 × 35.5 cm.)
Collection William McCarty-Cooper

87.
Graham Sutherland
Portrait of Douglas Cooper, 1966
Pencil and colored pencil on paper, $12\frac{1}{4} \times 9\frac{7}{8}$ in. (31 × 25 cm.)
Collection William McCarty-Cooper

ARTISTS' BIOGRAPHIES

GEORGES BRAQUE (1882–1963)

Georges Braque was born in Argenteuil near Paris and brought up on the coast of France in Le Havre. In 1900 he left for Paris and in 1902 he began his studies at the Académie Humbert, where he met fellow artists Marie Laurencin and Francis Picabia. In 1905 he saw Matisse's work in the Fauve room at the Salon d'Automne where his friends Othon Friesz and Raoul Dufy were also exhibiting. In 1906, after a summer of painting with Friesz in Antwerp and a winter in L'Estaque, Braque took on the brilliant colors of the Fauve artists in his painting. He subsequently exhibited with the Fauves at the 1907 Salon d'Automne and the Salon des Indépendants. That year Braque met Pablo Picasso; this began an intense working relationship between the two artists, out of which evolved the basic principles of Cubism. In 1908 Daniel-Henry Kahnweiler gave Braque his first solo exhibition, which consisted of works rejected by the Salon d'Automne. In his review of the exhibition at Kahnweiler's gallery, art critic Louis Vauxcelles described these works as a reduction of form into cubes. Reviewing Braque's works shown in the 1909 Salon des Indépendants, Vauxcelles found "bizarreries cubiques," and it was not long before the term "Cubism" came into general use. Braque's and Picasso's works from 1908 to 1912 have been identified as Analytic Cubism, where a subject's internal and external surfaces, as well as different viewpoints and perspectives, are brought together in a single composition. During these years Braque often played the role of innovator. In 1912, for example, he initiated experiments with *papiers collés* (compositions of pasted paper fragments). This innovation developed into what is known as Synthetic Cubism, in which the artist either combined fragments of material with drawing, or painted forms that imitated collage. Braque and Picasso worked together until Braque's mobilization in 1914 brought an end to their intense collaboration. After his convalescence from a severe head wound, Braque took up painting again in 1917, and by 1922 his work was the subject of a special exhibition at the Salon d'Automne in Paris. Important among his works of the 1920s was a series of classically-inspired *Canephores* — massive, partially draped women bearing fruit and flowers. The 1930s were the beginning of his preoccupation with the theme of the artist's studio. He also executed a large body of prints during this decade and these works exhibit his interest in classical Greek themes such as Hesiod's *Theogony.* His masterful later work was dominated to a great extent by still-life and interior themes. The monumental *Atelier* paintings of 1948 to 1955 offer an encyclopedic résumé of the stylistic innovations, the themes, and the motifs of his career. After Braque died in Paris in 1963, a state funeral was held at the Louvre.

JUAN GRIS (1887–1927)

Juan Gris was born José Victoriano Carmelo Carlos Gonzalez Pérez in Madrid. He began his art studies there in 1902 while he supported himself by providing drawings for various illustrated journals such as *Blanco y Negro.* Upon his move to Paris in 1906 he adopted the pseudonym Juan Gris. There he lived in the same building as Picasso, at 13, rue Ravignan, and became acquainted with the writers of the Paris avant-garde circle including Guillaume Apollinaire, André Salmon, and Max Jacob, who nicknamed the dilapidated house "Le Bateau-Lavoir" or "The Laundry Barge." Gris continued to make his living by submitting illustrations to various humor magazines such as *Papitú,* published in Barcelona, and *L'Assiette au Beurre,* published in Paris. His career as a painter began in earnest in 1910 with portraits and still lifes in a style based on the Analytic Cubism of Braque and Picasso. Gris, however, set his work apart from theirs: Braque and Picasso subjected concrete form to analysis, fragmentation, and abstraction, while Gris combined abstract fragments to make a cohesive form. In 1912 his work was exhibited in Barcelona at Galerias Dalmau, and in Paris at the Salon des Indépendants and the Salon de la Section d'Or, or Puteaux Group. He was allied with the Puteaux Cubists, who included Robert Delaunay, František Kupka, Fernand Léger, Jaques Villon, Marcel Duchamp, Raymond Duchamp-Villon, Albert Gleizes, Jean Metzinger, and Alexander Archipenko. This group emphasized color over the austere analysis of form found in the work of Braque and Picasso. About this time, Gris began to experiment with *papiers collés,* the collaged paper technique initiated by Braque, and Gris developed a personal but significant form of Synthetic Cubism. Also in 1912 he signed an exclusive contract with the important dealer and promoter of the Cubists, Daniel-Henry Kahnweiler. As a Spanish national, Gris was not required to fight in World War I, but he found himself in difficult financial straits during those years. For a time the important collector Gertrude Stein, who first purchased Gris's work in 1913, provided him with a monthly stipend in exchange for pictures; she later became a friend and collaborator. In 1917 Gris broke with Kahnweiler and allied himself with another important dealer of Cubism, Léonce Rosenberg. In 1919 his first important solo exhibition was held at Rosenberg's Galerie de l'Effort Moderne and in 1920 he exhibited at the last Cubist section of the Salon des Indépendants. In 1923 and 1925 Alfred Flechtheim exhibited his work in Berlin and Düsseldorf. During these years Gris was also active in set design and book illustration. Although, after years of ill health, Gris died in Boulogne-sur-Seine at the age of 40, he had already achieved a degree of recognition and had become one of Cubism's most articulate theoreticians. He noted in 1925, "If what has been called 'cubism' is only an appearance, then cubism has disappeared; if it is an aesthetic, then it has been absorbed into painting."

FERNAND LÉGER (1881–1955)

Fernand Léger was born in Normandy and he worked in Paris as an architectural draftsman from about 1900. In 1903 he began unofficially attending classes at the Ecole des Beaux Arts and at the Académie Julian. He was associated with the Cubists from 1910, and from 1911 he was a member of the Puteaux group, which included Jacques Villon, Juan Gris, and František Kupka. He exhibited with the Puteaux group in the Salon de la Section d'Or in 1912. At this time Léger's works tended toward a pure, nonfigurative abstraction, with the colors limited to the primaries and black and white. In 1913 he signed an exclusive contract with Daniel-Henry Kahnweiler and occupied himself with numerous abstract drawings and gouaches that treated the theme of "contrast of forms." He was mobilized in 1914 and, following his experiences at the front, Léger returned to a figurative mode. He expressed a sympathy for the working class and endeavored to create an art of proletarian subjects, accessible to all walks of life, in which he revealed with clarity and precision the beauty of everyday manufactured objects. His precise, clean style and his frequent depiction of industrial or machine elements also exemplify the Purist machine aesthetic promoted by Le Corbusier and Amédée Ozenfant in the 1920s. He also became active in theater during this time, producing stage and costume designs for *Skating Rink* in 1922 and for *La Création du monde* in 1923. He directed the first film without a plot, *Le Ballet mécanique*, in 1924. The following year he presented his first mural painting at Le Corbusier's pavillion of L'Esprit Nouveau at the Exposition des Arts Décoratifs in Paris. His achievements in theater design and his experimentation with film, as well as his enthusiasm for mural decoration, may be understood in terms of his desire to break away from conventional easel painting. In his work of the 1940s and 50s he depicted acrobats, cyclists, and workers in a monumental style, using heavy black outlines contrasted against free-floating areas of primary colors. Toward the end of his life he received many commissions for public works of art, including monumental figure paintings and murals — one commissioned by Douglas Cooper in 1954 — as well as ceramic decorations, tapestries, and windows. In 1960, five years after his death at Gif-sur-Yvette, the Musée National Fernand Léger was founded in Biot, France.

PABLO PICASSO (1881–1973)

Pablo Picasso was the dominant artistic personality of the twentieth century, and his work provided the impetus for many of the innovations of the first half of the century. He was born in Málaga, Andalusia. His father, an academic artist and teacher, encouraged his son's prodigious talent for painting and drawing. Picasso's first exhibition was held in 1900 in Barcelona, where his family had moved in 1895. He visited Paris frequently between 1900 and 1904; his work of this time has been called his Blue Period because of the dominant cold blue tonalities and the melancholic depictions of the outcasts of society. In 1904 Picasso moved to Paris, taking a studio in a run-down building at 13, rue Ravignan in Montmartre, dubbed by Max Jacob "Le Bateau-Lavoir," which soon evolved as a center of the avant-garde. In the autumn of 1905 Picasso sold his first works to Leo Stein and his sister Gertrude, initiating a long friendship between the artist and these important American collectors. In Picasso's work from 1905 to 1907, which has been called his Rose Period, the expressionistic passion of his early works gave way to more elegiac and romantic themes. Early in 1906 Ambroise Vollard, a gallery owner who would later become an important collector of Cubist art, purchased most of Picasso's Rose Period canvases. An exhibition of Iberian sculpture at the Louvre in 1906 and a visit in 1907 to the ethnographic museum at the Palais du Trocadéro inspired an abrupt change toward primitive stylization in his work of 1907 to 1909. Another important source for the stylization of figures in these paintings is Cézanne's analysis and simplification of forms. The *Demoiselles d'Avignon* is acknowledged as Picasso's masterpiece of this period, and a watershed work in the evolution of modern painting. From 1907 to 1914 Picasso worked closely with Georges Braque, evolving what has been termed Analytical Cubism, and from about 1912, Synthetic Cubism. The two artists sought to liberate art from the imitation of nature, addressing instead the basic elements of perception and pictorial notation. Techniques such as collage and *trompe l'oeil* took on important roles in this play with image and perception. Picasso, like Gris, was a Spanish citizen and was not involved in the war effort; this afforded him the opportunity to continue to develop and refine the techniques he and Braque had put into play in the preceding years. The 1920s saw an evolution from Synthetic Cubism to a monumental classical style. Picasso's work in the 1930s reveals the impact of Surrealism, and he even wrote and illustrated some Surealist poetry. He was the subject of two major retrospectives around this time, one in London in 1931 and one in Paris in 1932. During the 1930s he was active in printmaking, and between 1930 and 1937 Vollard acquired one hundred of these prints, which became known as the Vollard Suite. The subjects that preoccupied Picasso at this time, for example the artist in his studio and the minotaur, are evident in this group of prints. The Spanish Civil War forced the artist to become more active in politics, and in 1936, because of his opposition to General Franco, the Spanish Republicans made Picasso director of the Prado Museum. *Guernica*, his passionate condemnation of the bombing of a civilian population, was exhibited in the Spanish Pavilion at the Paris Exposition Universelle in 1937. During World War II Picasso lived primarily in Paris, but after the war he took up permanent residence in the South of France where he worked in painting, sculpture, and ceramics. His later works included a series of variations on Delacroix's *Femmes d'Algiers* and Manet's *Déjeuner sur l'herbe*, and in 1968 he produced the *347 Suite* of etchings. The vibrant creativity and evocative complexity of his last works has been recognized only relatively recently. Picasso was active until his death in Mougins at the age of 91.

Compiled by Shannon Halwes

SELECTED WRITINGS BY DOUGLAS COOPER

Organized by year of publication:

BOOKS

Juan Gris, ou le goût du solennel. Paris and Geneva: A. Skira, 1949.

Fernand Léger et le nouvel espace. London: Lund, Humphries, 1949; Geneva: Editions des Trois Collines, 1949. Text in French and English.

Fernand Léger: Dessins de guerre, 1915–1916. Paris: Berggruen & Cie, 1956.

Pablo Picasso: Carnet Catalan. Paris: Berggruen & Cie, 1958.

Pablo Picasso: Les Déjeuners. Paris: Editions Cercle d'Art, 1962. German edition, 1962; Spanish edition, 1962; American edition, 1963.

Picasso, théâtre. Paris: Editions Cercle d'Art, 1967. Italian edition, 1967; English edition, 1968; American edition, 1968; Spanish edition, 1968.

Pour Eugenia: Une Suite de 24 dessins inédits exécutés en 1918 par Pablo Picasso. Paris, Berggruen & Cie, 1976.

With the collaboration of Margaret Potter. *Juan Gris: Catalogue raisonné de l'oeuvre peint.* Paris, Berggruen & Cie, 1977.

EXHIBITION CATALOGUES

Fernand Léger: An Exhibition of Paintings, Drawings, Lithographs and Book Illustrations. London, The Tate Gallery, 1950.

Juan Gris. Bern, Kunstmuseum, 1956.

G. Braque. Organized by the Arts Council of Great Britain in association with the Edinburgh Festival Society. London, The Tate Gallery, 1956.

Picasso – dessins, gouaches, aquarelles, 1898–1957. Arles, Musée Reattu, 1957.

Picasso. Marseilles, Musée Cantini, 1959.

Georges Braque: Pradikat des ICOM: "agréée." Munich, Haus der Kunst, 1963.

Fernand Léger. Marseille, Musée Cantini, 1966.

Picasso, Two Concurrent Retrospective Exhibitions. Fort Worth: Fort Worth Art Center Museum; Dallas: Dallas Museum of Fine Arts, 1967.

The Cubist Epoch. Los Angeles County Museum of Art and the Metropolitan Museum of Art, New York; published London: Phiadon, 1970.

Braque: The Great Years. Chicago, The Art Institute, 1972. English edition, 1973.

Oeuvres cubistes: Braque, Gris, Léger, Picasso. Paris, Berggruen & Cie, 1973.

With Hans Albert Peters. *Juan Gris.* Baden-Baden, Kunsthalle, 1974.

Braque: The Papiers Collés. Washington, D.C., The National Gallery of Art, 1982. Includes essay, "Braque as Innovator: The First *'Papier Collé'*."

With Gary Tinterow. *The Essential Cubism: Braque, Picasso, and Their Friends, 1907–1920.* London: The Tate Gallery, 1983.